50 Desserts from Around the World Recipes for Home

By: Kelly Johnson

Table of Contents

- Tiramisu (Italy)
- Baklava (Turkey)
- Macarons (France)
- Churros with Chocolate Sauce (Spain)
- Cheesecake (United States)
- Mochi (Japan)
- Gulab Jamun (India)
- Pavlova (New Zealand)
- Pavé (Argentina)
- Kunafa (Middle East)
- Flan (Mexico)
- Cannoli (Italy)
- Pastel de Nata (Portugal)
- Creme Brulee (France)
- Lamingtons (Australia)
- Kheer (India)
- Baklava Cheesecake (Greece)
- Tres Leches Cake (Latin America)
- Strudel (Austria)
- Galette (France)
- Trifle (United Kingdom)
- Poffertjes (Netherlands)
- Loukoumades (Greece)
- Cannoli Cake (Italy)
- Brigadeiro (Brazil)
- Sacher Torte (Austria)
- Mille-Feuille (France)
- Sticky Toffee Pudding (United Kingdom)
- Mochi Ice Cream (Japan)
- Kulfi (India)
- Pavê de Chocolate (Brazil)
- Eclairs (France)
- Semla (Sweden)
- Cinnamon Rolls (Sweden)
- Sopapillas (Mexico)

- Bienenstich (Germany)
- Kaiserschmarrn (Austria)
- Alfajores (Argentina)
- Chocotorta (Argentina)
- Turkish Delight (Turkey)
- Bûche de Noël (France)
- Stroopwafel (Netherlands)
- Pandan Cake (Singapore)
- Basbousa (Middle East)
- Pumpkin Pie (United States)
- Maple Taffy (Canada)
- Peach Melba (Australia)
- Banoffee Pie (United Kingdom)
- Panna Cotta (Italy)
- Sufganiyah (Israel)

Tiramisu (Italy)

Ingredients:

- 6 large egg yolks
- 3/4 cup granulated sugar
- 1 cup mascarpone cheese, at room temperature
- 1 1/2 cups heavy cream
- 2 cups brewed strong coffee, cooled
- 1/4 cup coffee liqueur (optional)
- 1 teaspoon vanilla extract
- 2 packages ladyfingers (about 24-30 ladyfingers)
- Unsweetened cocoa powder, for dusting
- Chocolate shavings, for garnish (optional)

Instructions:

1. In a heatproof bowl, whisk together the egg yolks and sugar until well combined.
2. Place the bowl over a pot of simmering water (double boiler) and continue whisking constantly until the mixture thickens and becomes pale yellow, about 5-7 minutes.
3. Remove the bowl from heat and let it cool slightly.
4. Add the mascarpone cheese to the egg mixture and gently fold until smooth and well combined. Set aside.
5. In another bowl, whip the heavy cream until stiff peaks form.
6. Gently fold the whipped cream into the mascarpone mixture until smooth and creamy. Set aside.
7. In a shallow dish, combine the brewed coffee and coffee liqueur (if using).
8. Quickly dip each ladyfinger into the coffee mixture, ensuring they are soaked but not overly soggy.
9. Arrange a layer of soaked ladyfingers in the bottom of a 9x13-inch dish.
10. Spread half of the mascarpone mixture over the layer of ladyfingers, smoothing it out with a spatula.
11. Repeat the process with another layer of soaked ladyfingers and the remaining mascarpone mixture.
12. Cover the dish with plastic wrap and refrigerate for at least 4 hours, or preferably overnight, to allow the flavors to meld and the tiramisu to set.

13. Before serving, dust the top of the tiramisu with cocoa powder and garnish with chocolate shavings, if desired.
14. Slice and serve chilled. Enjoy your delicious homemade tiramisu!

Enjoy this classic Italian dessert with friends and family! Buon appetito!

Baklava (Turkey)

Ingredients:

For the Filling:

- 1 pound (about 4 cups) mixed nuts (such as walnuts, pistachios, and almonds), finely chopped
- 1/2 cup granulated sugar
- 1 teaspoon ground cinnamon
- 1/4 teaspoon ground cloves
- 1/4 teaspoon ground nutmeg
- 1/2 cup unsalted butter, melted

For the Syrup:

- 1 cup granulated sugar
- 1/2 cup water
- 1/2 cup honey
- 1 tablespoon lemon juice
- 1 cinnamon stick
- 4-5 whole cloves
- 1 teaspoon vanilla extract

For the Pastry:

- 1 package phyllo dough, thawed according to package instructions
- 1 cup unsalted butter, melted

Instructions:

1. Preheat your oven to 350°F (175°C). Lightly grease a 9x13-inch baking dish with butter.

2. In a mixing bowl, combine the chopped nuts, sugar, cinnamon, cloves, and nutmeg. Set aside.
3. Unroll the phyllo dough and cover it with a damp towel to prevent it from drying out.
4. Place one sheet of phyllo dough in the prepared baking dish and brush it generously with melted butter. Repeat with 7-8 more sheets, layering and buttering each sheet as you go.
5. Sprinkle about 1/3 of the nut mixture evenly over the layered phyllo dough.
6. Layer and butter another 7-8 sheets of phyllo dough on top of the nut mixture, repeating the process.
7. Continue layering and buttering phyllo dough and nut mixture until all of the nuts are used, finishing with a final layer of 7-8 sheets of phyllo dough on top.
8. Using a sharp knife, carefully cut the baklava into diamond or square-shaped pieces.
9. Bake in the preheated oven for 45-55 minutes, or until the baklava is golden brown and crisp.
10. While the baklava is baking, prepare the syrup. In a saucepan, combine the sugar, water, honey, lemon juice, cinnamon stick, and cloves. Bring to a boil over medium heat, then reduce the heat and simmer for 10-15 minutes, or until slightly thickened.
11. Remove the syrup from heat and stir in the vanilla extract. Let it cool slightly.
12. Once the baklava is done baking, remove it from the oven and immediately pour the cooled syrup evenly over the hot baklava, allowing it to soak in completely.
13. Allow the baklava to cool to room temperature before serving, allowing the flavors to develop fully.
14. Serve the baklava at room temperature and enjoy the delicious combination of crispy phyllo dough and sweet, nutty filling.

Baklava is best enjoyed fresh but can be stored in an airtight container at room temperature for several days. Enjoy this traditional Turkish dessert with a cup of hot tea or coffee! Afiyet olsun! (Bon Appétit!)

Macarons (France)

Ingredients:

For the Macaron Shells:

- 1 cup (100g) almond flour
- 1 3/4 cups (200g) powdered sugar
- 3 large egg whites, at room temperature
- Pinch of cream of tartar
- 1/4 cup (50g) granulated sugar
- Gel food coloring (optional)

For the Filling:

- Your choice of filling (e.g., buttercream, ganache, jam)

Instructions:

1. Prepare Baking Sheets: Line two baking sheets with parchment paper or silicone baking mats. You can also use a macaron template under the parchment paper to help guide you in piping evenly sized macarons.
2. Sift Dry Ingredients: In a medium bowl, sift together the almond flour and powdered sugar. Discard any large pieces of almond that remain in the sieve.
3. Whip Egg Whites: In a large, clean mixing bowl, beat the egg whites with an electric mixer on medium speed until frothy. Add a pinch of cream of tartar and continue beating until soft peaks form. Gradually add the granulated sugar, a spoonful at a time, while continuing to beat. Beat until stiff, glossy peaks form.
4. Macaronage: Gently fold the sifted dry ingredients into the whipped egg whites using a spatula. This step is called macaronage. Fold the mixture just until it reaches the ribbon stage, where it falls off the spatula in a ribbon and then disappears back into the batter after about 10-15 seconds.
5. Pipe Macaron Shells: Transfer the macaron batter to a piping bag fitted with a round tip. Pipe small circles onto the prepared baking sheets, leaving space between each one for spreading. If desired, you can gently tap the baking sheets on the counter to release any air bubbles. Let the piped macarons rest at room

temperature for about 30-60 minutes, until a skin forms on the surface and they are no longer sticky to the touch.
6. Preheat Oven: While the macarons are resting, preheat your oven to 300°F (150°C).
7. Bake: Once the macarons have formed a skin, bake them in the preheated oven for 12-15 minutes, rotating the baking sheets halfway through baking. The macarons are done when they are set and the tops are firm to the touch. Be careful not to overbake.
8. Cool: Remove the macarons from the oven and let them cool completely on the baking sheets before attempting to remove them.
9. Assemble: Once the macaron shells are completely cool, match them up into pairs of similar sizes. Pipe or spoon your desired filling onto the flat side of one macaron shell, then sandwich it with another shell, pressing gently to spread the filling to the edges.
10. Storage: Store the assembled macarons in an airtight container in the refrigerator for 24 hours to allow the flavors to meld. Bring them to room temperature before serving for the best texture and flavor.
11. Enjoy: Serve and enjoy these delicate and delicious French macarons!

Experiment with different flavors and colors to create a variety of macarons to suit your taste preferences. Bon appétit!

Churros with Chocolate Sauce (Spain)

Ingredients:

For the Churros:

- 1 cup water
- 2 tablespoons white sugar
- 1/2 teaspoon salt
- 2 tablespoons vegetable oil
- 1 cup all-purpose flour
- Vegetable oil, for frying

For the Cinnamon Sugar Coating:

- 1/2 cup granulated sugar
- 1 teaspoon ground cinnamon

For the Chocolate Sauce:

- 1 cup dark chocolate, chopped
- 1/2 cup heavy cream
- 1 tablespoon unsalted butter
- 1/2 teaspoon vanilla extract
- Pinch of salt

Instructions:

1. Prepare Chocolate Sauce: In a small saucepan, heat the heavy cream until it just begins to simmer. Remove from heat and add the chopped dark chocolate, butter, vanilla extract, and a pinch of salt. Stir until the chocolate and butter are melted and the sauce is smooth. Keep warm over low heat while you make the churros.

2. Make Churro Dough: In a medium saucepan, combine the water, sugar, salt, and 2 tablespoons of vegetable oil. Bring the mixture to a boil over medium-high heat. Remove from heat and stir in the flour until the mixture forms a dough.
3. Fry Churros: Heat vegetable oil in a deep fryer or heavy-bottomed pot to 375°F (190°C). Transfer the churro dough to a piping bag fitted with a star tip. Pipe 4-inch strips of dough directly into the hot oil, using scissors to cut them off. Fry the churros until they are golden brown and crisp, about 2-3 minutes per side. Use a slotted spoon to remove the fried churros and drain them on paper towels.
4. Coat with Cinnamon Sugar: In a shallow dish, combine the granulated sugar and ground cinnamon. Roll the warm churros in the cinnamon sugar mixture until evenly coated.
5. Serve: Serve the warm churros immediately with the chocolate sauce for dipping.
6. Enjoy: Enjoy these crispy, cinnamon-sugar-coated churros with rich, decadent chocolate sauce as a delicious treat any time of day!

Churros are best enjoyed fresh, but any leftovers can be stored in an airtight container at room temperature and reheated in the oven for a few minutes to crisp them up again.

¡Buen provecho! (Enjoy your meal!)

Cheesecake (United States)

Ingredients:

For the Crust:

- 1 1/2 cups graham cracker crumbs (about 10-12 whole graham crackers)
- 1/4 cup granulated sugar
- 1/2 cup unsalted butter, melted

For the Filling:

- 4 (8-ounce) packages cream cheese, softened
- 1 1/4 cups granulated sugar
- 4 large eggs
- 1/4 cup sour cream
- 1/4 cup heavy cream
- 1 tablespoon vanilla extract
- 2 tablespoons all-purpose flour

For the Topping (Optional):

- Fresh fruit (strawberries, blueberries, raspberries)
- Fruit preserves or sauce
- Whipped cream

Instructions:

1. Preheat Oven: Preheat your oven to 325°F (160°C). Grease a 9-inch springform pan with butter or non-stick cooking spray.
2. Make Crust: In a mixing bowl, combine the graham cracker crumbs, sugar, and melted butter. Press the mixture firmly and evenly into the bottom of the prepared springform pan.

3. Bake Crust: Bake the crust in the preheated oven for 10 minutes. Remove from the oven and let it cool while you prepare the filling.
4. Make Filling: In a large mixing bowl, beat the cream cheese and sugar together until smooth and creamy. Add the eggs one at a time, beating well after each addition. Scrape down the sides of the bowl as needed.
5. Add Sour Cream and Heavy Cream: Mix in the sour cream, heavy cream, and vanilla extract until well combined. Stir in the flour until smooth.
6. Pour Filling: Pour the cheesecake filling over the cooled crust in the springform pan. Smooth out the top with a spatula.
7. Bake Cheesecake: Place the cheesecake in the preheated oven and bake for 60-70 minutes, or until the edges are set but the center is still slightly wobbly.
8. Cool and Chill: Turn off the oven and leave the cheesecake inside with the door slightly ajar for about 1 hour to cool gradually. Remove the cheesecake from the oven and let it cool completely at room temperature. Once cooled, cover the cheesecake with plastic wrap and refrigerate for at least 4 hours, or preferably overnight, to set.
9. Serve: When ready to serve, release the cheesecake from the springform pan and transfer it to a serving platter. If desired, top with fresh fruit, fruit preserves or sauce, and whipped cream.
10. Slice and Enjoy: Slice the cheesecake into wedges and serve chilled. Enjoy the creamy and indulgent flavor of this classic New York cheesecake!

Leftover cheesecake can be stored covered in the refrigerator for up to 5 days. Bring it to room temperature before serving for the best texture and flavor.

Mochi (Japan)

Ingredients:

- 1 cup mochiko (glutinous rice flour)
- 1 cup water
- 1/4 cup granulated sugar (adjust to taste)
- Cornstarch or potato starch (for dusting)

Optional Fillings:

- Sweet red bean paste (anko)
- Fresh fruit (strawberries, mango, etc.)
- Ice cream

Instructions:

1. Prepare Steamer: If you have a steamer, line it with a clean cloth or parchment paper. If you don't have a steamer, fill a large pot with water and place a rack or steaming basket inside, ensuring that the water doesn't touch the bottom of the steaming vessel. Cover the pot and bring the water to a boil.
2. Mix Dough: In a microwave-safe bowl, combine the mochiko, water, and sugar. Stir until smooth and well combined.
3. Microwave Method: Cover the bowl loosely with plastic wrap and microwave on high for 2-3 minutes. Remove from the microwave and stir well. Return to the microwave and cook for an additional 1-2 minutes until the dough is thick and sticky.
4. Steam Method: Pour the mochiko mixture into the prepared steamer or onto a plate lined with parchment paper. Steam for 20-25 minutes, or until the dough is cooked through and no longer sticky.
5. Shape Mochi: While the mochi is still warm, dust a clean work surface with cornstarch or potato starch. Transfer the mochi onto the dusted surface. Be careful as the mochi will be hot. Use a spatula or wooden spoon to fold and knead the mochi until it becomes smooth and elastic.
6. Forming Mochi Balls: Divide the mochi into equal portions and shape each portion into a small ball. Flatten each ball with your fingers to form a disc.

7. Fill Mochi (Optional): Place a small amount of sweet red bean paste, fresh fruit, or ice cream in the center of each mochi disc. Fold the edges of the mochi over the filling and pinch to seal.
8. Serve: Serve the mochi immediately or store them in an airtight container at room temperature for up to 2 days. If storing, dust the mochi with additional cornstarch or potato starch to prevent sticking.
9. Enjoy: Enjoy the delicious and chewy texture of homemade Japanese mochi with your favorite fillings!

Mochi is a versatile treat and can be enjoyed in various ways. Experiment with different fillings and flavors to create your own unique mochi creations. Enjoy!

Gulab Jamun (India)

Ingredients:

For the Gulab Jamun:

- 1 cup milk powder
- 1/4 cup all-purpose flour
- 1/4 teaspoon baking soda
- 2 tablespoons ghee (clarified butter), melted
- 3-4 tablespoons milk (approximately)
- Oil or ghee for frying

For the Sugar Syrup:

- 1 1/2 cups granulated sugar
- 1 1/2 cups water
- 4-5 green cardamom pods, crushed
- 1 teaspoon rose water or kewra water (optional)
- Saffron strands (optional)
- Chopped nuts (pistachios, almonds) for garnish

Instructions:

1. Prepare Sugar Syrup: In a saucepan, combine the granulated sugar, water, and crushed cardamom pods. Bring the mixture to a boil over medium heat, stirring until the sugar is completely dissolved. Reduce the heat to low and simmer for about 5-7 minutes to thicken slightly. Remove from heat and stir in the rose water or kewra water (if using) and saffron strands. Keep the sugar syrup warm while you prepare the gulab jamun.
2. Make Gulab Jamun Dough: In a mixing bowl, combine the milk powder, all-purpose flour, and baking soda. Gradually add the melted ghee and mix until the mixture resembles coarse crumbs. Slowly add the milk, a tablespoon at a time, and knead until a soft and smooth dough forms. Be careful not to over-knead the dough.

3. Shape Gulab Jamun: Divide the dough into small equal-sized portions and roll each portion into smooth balls without any cracks. Make sure the balls are smooth and without cracks to prevent them from breaking while frying.
4. Fry Gulab Jamun: Heat oil or ghee in a deep frying pan or kadhai over medium-low heat. Once the oil is hot, carefully add the prepared gulab jamun balls in batches, making sure not to overcrowd the pan. Fry the gulab jamun balls, stirring gently and occasionally, until they turn golden brown and evenly cooked on all sides. Adjust the heat as needed to maintain a gentle simmer to avoid burning.
5. Soak Gulab Jamun: Once fried, remove the gulab jamun balls from the oil using a slotted spoon and immediately transfer them to the warm sugar syrup. Allow the gulab jamun to soak in the syrup for at least 1-2 hours or until they are soft, spongy, and well-soaked.
6. Serve: Garnish the gulab jamun with chopped nuts (pistachios, almonds) before serving. Serve warm or at room temperature, allowing the flavors to meld and the gulab jamun to absorb the syrup fully.
7. Enjoy: Enjoy these delicious, melt-in-your-mouth gulab jamun as a sweet treat for special occasions or festive celebrations!

Gulab jamun can be stored in the refrigerator for up to a week. Reheat them gently before serving to enjoy them warm and soft. Enjoy!

Pavlova (New Zealand)

Ingredients:

For the Pavlova:

- 4 large egg whites, at room temperature
- 1 cup granulated sugar
- 1 teaspoon white vinegar or lemon juice
- 1 teaspoon cornstarch (cornflour)
- 1/2 teaspoon vanilla extract
- Pinch of salt

For the Topping:

- 1 cup heavy cream
- 1 tablespoon powdered sugar (confectioners' sugar)
- Fresh fruit (such as strawberries, kiwi, passionfruit, or berries)
- Mint leaves for garnish (optional)

Instructions:

1. Preheat Oven: Preheat your oven to 300°F (150°C). Line a baking sheet with parchment paper and draw a 9-inch circle on the parchment paper as a guide for shaping the pavlova.
2. Make Pavlova Base: In a clean, dry mixing bowl, beat the egg whites with an electric mixer on medium speed until soft peaks form. Gradually add the granulated sugar, one tablespoon at a time, while continuing to beat on high speed. Beat until the mixture is glossy and stiff peaks form. This process may take about 8-10 minutes.
3. Add Vinegar and Cornstarch: Gently fold in the vinegar or lemon juice, cornstarch, vanilla extract, and a pinch of salt until well combined.
4. Shape Pavlova: Spoon the pavlova mixture onto the prepared baking sheet, using the drawn circle as a guide. Use a spatula to spread the mixture evenly within the circle, creating a slight indentation in the center for holding the toppings.
5. Bake Pavlova: Place the pavlova in the preheated oven and immediately reduce the temperature to 250°F (120°C). Bake for 1 hour and 15 minutes to 1 hour and

30 minutes, or until the pavlova is crisp on the outside and dry to the touch. The center should be soft and marshmallow-like.
6. Cool Pavlova: Turn off the oven and let the pavlova cool completely inside the oven with the door slightly ajar. This helps prevent cracking.
7. Prepare Topping: In a mixing bowl, whip the heavy cream and powdered sugar until stiff peaks form.
8. Assemble Pavlova: Once the pavlova has cooled, carefully transfer it to a serving platter or cake stand. Spoon the whipped cream onto the center of the pavlova and spread it out evenly. Arrange the fresh fruit on top of the whipped cream.
9. Garnish and Serve: Garnish the pavlova with mint leaves, if desired. Serve immediately, slicing the pavlova into wedges, and enjoy!

Pavlova is best enjoyed fresh on the day it is made. Leftovers can be stored in an airtight container in the refrigerator for up to 2 days, but note that the texture may soften slightly. Enjoy this iconic New Zealand dessert with friends and family!

Pavé (Argentina)

Ingredients:

For the Cake:

- 2 cups (250g) all-purpose flour
- 1 cup (200g) granulated sugar
- 1/2 cup (50g) unsweetened cocoa powder
- 1 teaspoon baking powder
- 1/2 teaspoon baking soda
- 1/2 teaspoon salt
- 1/2 cup (120ml) vegetable oil
- 2 large eggs
- 1 teaspoon vanilla extract
- 1 cup (240ml) strong brewed coffee, cooled

For the Filling:

- 2 cups (480ml) heavy cream
- 1/4 cup (50g) granulated sugar
- 1 teaspoon vanilla extract

For the Chocolate Ganache:

- 1 cup (180g) semisweet chocolate chips
- 1/2 cup (120ml) heavy cream
- 1 tablespoon unsalted butter

Instructions:

1. Preheat Oven: Preheat your oven to 350°F (175°C). Grease a 9x9-inch square baking pan and line it with parchment paper, leaving an overhang on two sides for easy removal.

2. **Make Cake:** In a large mixing bowl, sift together the flour, sugar, cocoa powder, baking powder, baking soda, and salt. In another bowl, whisk together the vegetable oil, eggs, vanilla extract, and cooled brewed coffee. Gradually add the wet ingredients to the dry ingredients, stirring until just combined. Pour the batter into the prepared baking pan and spread it out evenly.
3. **Bake Cake:** Bake in the preheated oven for 25-30 minutes, or until a toothpick inserted into the center comes out clean. Remove the cake from the oven and let it cool completely in the pan on a wire rack.
4. **Make Filling:** In a mixing bowl, whip the heavy cream, sugar, and vanilla extract until stiff peaks form.
5. **Assemble Pavé:** Once the cake has cooled completely, carefully remove it from the pan using the parchment paper overhang. Cut the cake in half horizontally to create two thin layers. Place one layer of cake back into the bottom of the pan. Spread the whipped cream filling evenly over the cake layer. Place the second layer of cake on top of the filling.
6. **Make Ganache:** In a small saucepan, heat the heavy cream until it just begins to simmer. Remove from heat and add the semisweet chocolate chips and butter. Let it sit for a minute, then stir until smooth and glossy.
7. **Top with Ganache:** Pour the chocolate ganache over the top layer of cake, spreading it out evenly with a spatula.
8. **Chill:** Cover the pan with plastic wrap and refrigerate the pavé for at least 4 hours, or preferably overnight, to set.
9. **Serve:** Once set, use the parchment paper overhang to lift the pavé out of the pan. Slice it into squares and serve chilled. Enjoy this rich and decadent Argentinean dessert!

Pavé is best enjoyed cold and can be stored covered in the refrigerator for up to 3 days.

Enjoy this indulgent treat with friends and family!

Kunafa (Middle East)

Ingredients:

For the Kunafa Dough:

- 1 pound (450g) kataifi dough (shredded phyllo dough)
- 1 cup (225g) unsalted butter, melted

For the Cheese Filling:

- 2 cups (450g) akkawi cheese or mozzarella cheese, shredded
- 1/2 cup (120ml) heavy cream
- 1 tablespoon granulated sugar (optional)

For the Sugar Syrup:

- 1 cup (240ml) water
- 1 cup (200g) granulated sugar
- 1 tablespoon lemon juice
- 1 tablespoon rose water or orange blossom water

For Garnish (Optional):

- Chopped pistachios or almonds

Instructions:

1. Prepare Sugar Syrup: In a saucepan, combine the water, sugar, and lemon juice. Bring the mixture to a boil over medium heat, stirring until the sugar is completely dissolved. Reduce the heat to low and simmer for about 10 minutes, or until the syrup thickens slightly. Remove from heat and stir in the rose water or orange blossom water. Set aside to cool.

2. **Prepare Cheese Filling:** In a mixing bowl, combine the shredded akkawi cheese or mozzarella cheese with the heavy cream and granulated sugar (if using). Mix until well combined and set aside.
3. **Assemble Kunafa:**
   - Preheat your oven to 350°F (175°C). Grease a 9x13-inch baking dish with butter.
   - Place the kataifi dough in a large mixing bowl and separate the strands with your fingers to loosen them.
   - Pour the melted butter over the kataifi dough and toss until evenly coated.
   - Press half of the buttered kataifi dough into the bottom of the prepared baking dish, pressing it down firmly to create an even layer.
   - Spread the cheese filling evenly over the bottom layer of kataifi dough.
   - Cover the cheese filling with the remaining buttered kataifi dough, pressing it down gently.
4. **Bake Kunafa:** Place the baking dish in the preheated oven and bake for 35-40 minutes, or until the kunafa is golden brown and crispy.
5. **Syrup and Garnish:**
   - Once baked, remove the kunafa from the oven and immediately pour the cooled sugar syrup evenly over the hot kunafa, allowing it to soak in completely.
   - Garnish the kunafa with chopped pistachios or almonds, if desired.
6. **Serve:** Allow the kunafa to cool slightly before slicing it into squares or wedges. Serve warm or at room temperature, drizzling any remaining sugar syrup over each serving.
7. **Enjoy:** Enjoy this delicious and indulgent Middle Eastern dessert with friends and family!

Kunafa is best enjoyed fresh on the day it is made. Leftovers can be stored in an airtight container in the refrigerator for up to 2 days, but note that the texture may soften slightly. Reheat gently in the oven before serving, if desired. Enjoy!

Flan (Mexico)

Ingredients:

For the Caramel:

- 1 cup (200g) granulated sugar
- 1/4 cup water

For the Custard:

- 4 large eggs
- 1 can (14 ounces) sweetened condensed milk
- 1 can (12 ounces) evaporated milk
- 1 teaspoon vanilla extract

Instructions:

1. Preheat Oven: Preheat your oven to 350°F (175°C).
2. Prepare Caramel: In a small saucepan, combine the granulated sugar and water over medium heat. Stir until the sugar is dissolved. Once dissolved, stop stirring and let the mixture cook, swirling the pan occasionally, until it turns a deep amber color, about 10-12 minutes. Be careful not to let it burn. Immediately pour the caramel into a 9-inch round baking dish, tilting the dish to coat the bottom evenly. Set aside to cool and harden.
3. Make Custard: In a mixing bowl, whisk together the eggs, sweetened condensed milk, evaporated milk, and vanilla extract until smooth and well combined.
4. Pour Custard Mixture: Once the caramel has cooled and hardened in the baking dish, pour the custard mixture over the caramel.
5. Bake Flan: Place the baking dish in a larger roasting pan or baking dish. Create a water bath by filling the larger pan with hot water until it reaches about halfway up the sides of the baking dish containing the flan mixture. Carefully transfer the water bath and flan to the preheated oven and bake for 50-60 minutes, or until the flan is set but still slightly jiggly in the center.

6. Chill and Serve: Remove the flan from the water bath and let it cool to room temperature. Once cooled, cover the baking dish with plastic wrap and refrigerate the flan for at least 4 hours, or preferably overnight, to chill and set completely.
7. Serve: To serve, run a knife around the edge of the baking dish to loosen the flan. Place a serving plate upside down on top of the baking dish and quickly flip it over to invert the flan onto the plate. The caramel sauce will flow over the top of the flan. Slice and serve chilled.
8. Enjoy: Enjoy this creamy and decadent Mexican dessert with its caramelized sweetness and silky smooth texture!

Flan can be stored covered in the refrigerator for up to 3 days. Serve it chilled for the best taste and texture. Enjoy!

Cannoli (Italy)

Ingredients:

For the Cannoli Shells:

- 2 cups (250g) all-purpose flour
- 2 tablespoons granulated sugar
- 1/4 teaspoon salt
- 2 tablespoons unsalted butter, softened
- 1/2 cup Marsala wine or white wine
- 1 egg white, lightly beaten (for sealing)
- Vegetable oil, for frying

For the Cannoli Filling:

- 2 cups (475g) ricotta cheese, drained
- 1/2 cup (60g) powdered sugar, plus more for dusting
- 1 teaspoon vanilla extract
- 1/4 cup mini chocolate chips
- Candied fruit or chopped nuts (optional, for garnish)

Instructions:

1. Make Cannoli Dough:
    - In a mixing bowl, sift together the flour, granulated sugar, and salt.
    - Add the softened butter to the dry ingredients and mix until crumbly.
    - Gradually add the Marsala wine, mixing until a dough forms. Knead the dough on a lightly floured surface until smooth and elastic, about 5-7 minutes. Wrap the dough in plastic wrap and let it rest at room temperature for 30 minutes.
2. Roll and Cut Dough:
    - Divide the dough into two equal portions. On a lightly floured surface, roll out one portion of the dough until it is very thin, about 1/8 inch thick. Using a 4-inch round cookie cutter or a glass, cut out circles from the dough.

- Repeat the process with the remaining dough, rerolling scraps as needed.
3. Shape Cannoli Shells:
    - Wrap each dough circle around a metal cannoli tube, overlapping the edges slightly. Brush the edge with the beaten egg white and press to seal.
    - Heat vegetable oil in a deep fryer or heavy-bottomed pot to 350°F (175°C). Fry the cannoli shells in batches, turning occasionally, until golden brown and crisp, about 2-3 minutes per batch.
    - Using tongs, carefully remove the fried cannoli shells from the oil and transfer them to a wire rack or paper towels to drain and cool completely.
4. Make Cannoli Filling:
    - In a mixing bowl, combine the drained ricotta cheese, powdered sugar, and vanilla extract. Mix until smooth and creamy. Stir in the mini chocolate chips.
    - Cover and refrigerate the cannoli filling for at least 1 hour to allow the flavors to meld.
5. Fill Cannoli Shells:
    - When ready to serve, fill a piping bag fitted with a large star tip with the chilled cannoli filling. Pipe the filling into each end of the cooled cannoli shells, filling them completely.
    - If desired, garnish the ends of the cannoli with candied fruit or chopped nuts.
6. Serve: Dust the filled cannoli with powdered sugar just before serving. Arrange them on a serving platter and enjoy immediately!

Cannoli are best enjoyed fresh, but any leftovers can be stored in an airtight container in the refrigerator for up to 2 days. Enjoy these delicious Italian treats with friends and family! Buon appetito!

Pastel de Nata (Portugal)

Ingredients:

For the Pastry:

- 1 sheet of puff pastry, thawed (store-bought or homemade)

For the Custard Filling:

- 1 cup (240ml) whole milk
- 3/4 cup (150g) granulated sugar
- 1 cinnamon stick
- Peel of 1/2 lemon
- 2 tablespoons all-purpose flour
- 2 tablespoons cornstarch
- 6 large egg yolks
- 1 teaspoon vanilla extract

For Dusting:

- Powdered sugar (optional)
- Ground cinnamon (optional)

Instructions:

1. Preheat Oven: Preheat your oven to 475°F (245°C). Grease a standard muffin tin or tart molds with butter or cooking spray.
2. Prepare Pastry: Roll out the puff pastry on a lightly floured surface until it is about 1/8 inch thick. Using a round cutter slightly larger than the muffin tin cups, cut out circles of pastry dough. Press each dough circle into the prepared muffin tin cups, gently pressing the dough up the sides.
3. Make Custard Filling:

- In a saucepan, combine the whole milk, granulated sugar, cinnamon stick, and lemon peel. Heat over medium heat until the mixture begins to simmer, stirring occasionally to dissolve the sugar.
- In a separate bowl, whisk together the all-purpose flour, cornstarch, egg yolks, and vanilla extract until smooth.
- Once the milk mixture is simmering, remove the cinnamon stick and lemon peel. Gradually whisk in the egg yolk mixture, whisking constantly to prevent lumps from forming.
- Cook the custard mixture over medium heat, stirring constantly, until it thickens and coats the back of a spoon, about 5-7 minutes. Remove from heat and let the custard cool slightly.

4. Fill Pastry Cups: Spoon the slightly cooled custard filling into the prepared pastry cups, filling them about 3/4 full.
5. Bake: Place the filled muffin tin in the preheated oven and bake for 12-15 minutes, or until the pastry is golden brown and the custard is set with a slightly caramelized top.
6. Cool and Serve: Remove the pastéis de nata from the oven and let them cool in the muffin tin for a few minutes before transferring them to a wire rack to cool completely. Once cooled, dust with powdered sugar and ground cinnamon, if desired.
7. Enjoy: Serve these delightful Portuguese custard tarts at room temperature or slightly warmed. They are best enjoyed on the day they are made but can be stored in an airtight container in the refrigerator for up to 2 days. Enjoy the creamy custard and flaky pastry of pastel de nata as a delightful treat!

Pastéis de nata are a beloved Portuguese pastry enjoyed by locals and visitors alike. Their creamy custard filling and flaky pastry crust make them a delightful indulgence any time of day. Bom apetite!

Creme Brulee (France)

Ingredients:

- 4 large egg yolks
- 1/4 cup (50g) granulated sugar, plus extra for caramelizing
- 1 teaspoon vanilla extract
- 1 cup (240ml) heavy cream
- 1/2 cup (120ml) whole milk
- Pinch of salt

Instructions:

1. Preheat Oven: Preheat your oven to 325°F (160°C). Place four ramekins in a baking dish or roasting pan.
2. Prepare Custard Mixture: In a mixing bowl, whisk together the egg yolks, granulated sugar, and vanilla extract until well combined and slightly pale in color.
3. Heat Cream and Milk: In a saucepan, heat the heavy cream, whole milk, and a pinch of salt over medium heat until it just begins to simmer. Do not boil.
4. Temper Eggs: Slowly pour the hot cream mixture into the egg yolk mixture, whisking constantly, to temper the eggs and prevent them from curdling.
5. Strain Mixture: Strain the custard mixture through a fine-mesh sieve into a clean bowl to remove any lumps or air bubbles.
6. Fill Ramekins: Divide the custard mixture evenly among the prepared ramekins.
7. Bake: Pour hot water into the baking dish or roasting pan until it reaches halfway up the sides of the ramekins, creating a water bath. Carefully transfer the baking dish to the preheated oven and bake for 30-35 minutes, or until the custard is set around the edges but still slightly jiggly in the center.
8. Chill: Remove the ramekins from the water bath and let them cool to room temperature. Then, cover them with plastic wrap and refrigerate for at least 4 hours, or preferably overnight, to chill and set completely.
9. Caramelize Sugar: Just before serving, sprinkle a thin, even layer of granulated sugar over the top of each chilled custard. Use a kitchen torch to caramelize the sugar until it forms a golden-brown crust.
10. Serve: Let the crème brûlée sit for a minute to allow the caramelized sugar to harden, then serve immediately.

11. Enjoy: Enjoy the creamy, indulgent texture and the contrasting crisp caramelized sugar crust of this classic French dessert!

Crème brûlée is best served fresh, but any leftovers can be stored in the refrigerator for up to 2 days. Enjoy this elegant dessert on special occasions or anytime you crave a luxurious treat!

Lamingtons (Australia)

Ingredients:

For the Cake:

- 2 cups (250g) all-purpose flour
- 2 teaspoons baking powder
- 1/4 teaspoon salt
- 1/2 cup (115g) unsalted butter, softened
- 1 cup (200g) granulated sugar
- 2 large eggs
- 1 teaspoon vanilla extract
- 1/2 cup (120ml) milk

For the Chocolate Coating:

- 3 cups (360g) powdered sugar (confectioners' sugar)
- 1/3 cup (30g) unsweetened cocoa powder
- 1/2 cup (120ml) milk
- 2 tablespoons unsalted butter
- 2 cups (200g) desiccated coconut, for coating

Instructions:

1. Preheat Oven and Prepare Pan: Preheat your oven to 350°F (175°C). Grease and line a 9x13-inch baking pan with parchment paper, leaving an overhang on two sides for easy removal.
2. Make Cake: In a mixing bowl, sift together the all-purpose flour, baking powder, and salt. In another bowl, cream together the softened butter and granulated sugar until light and fluffy. Add the eggs one at a time, beating well after each addition. Stir in the vanilla extract. Gradually add the dry ingredients to the wet ingredients, alternating with the milk, and mix until well combined.
3. Bake Cake: Pour the cake batter into the prepared baking pan and spread it out evenly. Bake in the preheated oven for 25-30 minutes, or until a toothpick inserted into the center comes out clean. Remove from the oven and let the cake cool completely in the pan.

4. **Prepare Chocolate Coating:** In a saucepan, combine the powdered sugar, unsweetened cocoa powder, milk, and unsalted butter. Cook over low heat, stirring constantly, until the mixture is smooth and well combined. Remove from heat and let it cool slightly.
5. **Assemble Lamingtons:** Once the cake has cooled completely, lift it out of the pan using the parchment paper overhang and place it on a cutting board. Cut the cake into squares or rectangles, about 2x2 inches in size.
6. **Coat with Chocolate and Coconut:** Dip each cake piece into the chocolate coating mixture, ensuring it is fully coated. Let any excess chocolate drip off, then roll the coated cake in desiccated coconut until evenly coated. Place the coated lamingtons on a wire rack to set.
7. **Chill and Serve:** Once all the lamingtons are coated, place them in the refrigerator for about 30 minutes to allow the chocolate coating to set.
8. **Enjoy:** Serve these delicious Australian lamingtons as a sweet treat for dessert or snack time!

Lamingtons are best enjoyed fresh but can be stored in an airtight container at room temperature for up to 3 days. Enjoy the light and fluffy cake coated in rich chocolate and desiccated coconut for a delightful indulgence!

Kheer (India)

Ingredients:

- 1/2 cup (100g) basmati rice
- 4 cups (960ml) whole milk
- 1/2 cup (100g) granulated sugar (adjust to taste)
- 1/4 cup (30g) chopped nuts (almonds, cashews, pistachios, etc.)
- 1 tablespoon raisins
- 1/2 teaspoon ground cardamom
- Pinch of saffron strands (optional)
- Rose water or kewra water (optional)
- Silvered almonds and pistachios for garnish

Instructions:

1. Rinse Rice: Rinse the basmati rice under cold water until the water runs clear. Drain well.
2. Cook Rice: In a saucepan, combine the rinsed rice and whole milk. Bring the mixture to a gentle boil over medium heat, stirring frequently to prevent the rice from sticking to the bottom of the pan.
3. Simmer: Once the mixture comes to a boil, reduce the heat to low and let it simmer uncovered, stirring occasionally, until the rice is tender and the mixture has thickened to a creamy consistency. This may take about 30-40 minutes.
4. Add Sugar and Nuts: Stir in the granulated sugar, chopped nuts, raisins, ground cardamom, and saffron strands (if using). Continue to simmer for another 5-10 minutes, stirring occasionally, until the sugar is dissolved and the nuts and raisins are well incorporated.
5. Flavor with Rose Water or Kewra Water: If using, stir in a few drops of rose water or kewra water to add fragrance to the kheer. Be careful not to add too much, as these flavors can be overpowering.
6. Serve: Remove the kheer from heat and let it cool slightly. Serve warm or chilled, garnished with slivered almonds and pistachios.
7. Enjoy: Enjoy this creamy and aromatic Indian rice pudding as a delightful dessert or sweet treat!

Kheer can be served warm, at room temperature, or chilled, depending on your preference. Leftovers can be stored in an airtight container in the refrigerator for up to 3 days. Reheat gently before serving, if desired. Enjoy the rich and comforting flavors of homemade kheer with your loved ones!

Baklava Cheesecake (Greece)

Ingredients:

For the Baklava Layer:

- 1 cup (225g) unsalted butter, melted
- 1 pound (450g) phyllo dough, thawed according to package instructions
- 1 1/2 cups (180g) chopped nuts (such as walnuts, pistachios, or almonds)
- 1/2 cup (100g) granulated sugar
- 1 teaspoon ground cinnamon
- 1/2 teaspoon ground cloves
- 1/2 cup (120ml) honey
- 1/4 cup (60ml) water
- 1 teaspoon lemon juice
- 1 teaspoon vanilla extract

For the Cheesecake Layer:

- 24 ounces (680g) cream cheese, softened
- 1 cup (200g) granulated sugar
- 1 teaspoon vanilla extract
- 4 large eggs
- 1/4 cup (60ml) sour cream
- 1/4 cup (60ml) heavy cream

For Garnish (Optional):

- Chopped nuts (walnuts, pistachios, or almonds)
- Honey

Instructions:

1. Preheat Oven: Preheat your oven to 325°F (160°C). Grease a 9-inch springform pan with butter or non-stick cooking spray.
2. Prepare Baklava Layer:

- In a mixing bowl, combine the chopped nuts, granulated sugar, ground cinnamon, and ground cloves. Set aside.
- In another bowl, mix together the honey, water, lemon juice, and vanilla extract. Set aside.
- Lay a sheet of phyllo dough in the prepared springform pan, letting the excess hang over the edges. Brush the phyllo sheet with melted butter. Repeat layering with half of the phyllo sheets, brushing each layer with melted butter.
- Sprinkle half of the nut mixture evenly over the layered phyllo sheets.
- Continue layering the remaining phyllo sheets on top, brushing each layer with melted butter. Sprinkle the remaining nut mixture evenly over the top layer.
- Using a sharp knife, carefully cut the overhanging edges of the phyllo dough to fit the pan.

3. Bake Baklava Layer: Place the springform pan on a baking sheet to catch any drips. Bake in the preheated oven for 40-45 minutes, or until the baklava layer is golden brown and crisp. Remove from the oven and let it cool slightly.
4. Prepare Cheesecake Layer:
   - In a large mixing bowl, beat the cream cheese, granulated sugar, and vanilla extract until smooth and creamy.
   - Add the eggs one at a time, mixing well after each addition.
   - Stir in the sour cream and heavy cream until well combined.
5. Assemble Cheesecake:
   - Pour the cheesecake batter over the slightly cooled baklava layer in the springform pan, spreading it out evenly.
6. Bake Cheesecake: Return the springform pan to the oven and bake for 55-60 minutes, or until the cheesecake is set around the edges but slightly jiggly in the center.
7. Chill and Garnish:
   - Remove the cheesecake from the oven and let it cool to room temperature in the pan.
   - Once cooled, refrigerate the cheesecake for at least 4 hours, or preferably overnight, to chill and set completely.
   - Before serving, garnish the cheesecake with chopped nuts and drizzle with honey, if desired.
8. Slice and Serve: Release the sides of the springform pan and transfer the cheesecake to a serving platter. Slice into wedges and serve chilled.

9. Enjoy: Enjoy the delicious fusion of baklava and cheesecake, with its layers of crisp phyllo pastry, sweet nut filling, and creamy cheesecake. It's a delightful treat for any occasion!

This baklava cheesecake can be stored covered in the refrigerator for up to 3 days. Enjoy this indulgent dessert with friends and family!

Tres Leches Cake (Latin America)

Ingredients:

For the Cake:

- 1 cup (125g) all-purpose flour
- 1 1/2 teaspoons baking powder
- 1/4 teaspoon salt
- 4 large eggs, separated
- 1 cup (200g) granulated sugar, divided
- 1/3 cup (80ml) whole milk
- 1 teaspoon vanilla extract

For the Three Milks Mixture:

- 1 can (12 ounces / 354ml) evaporated milk
- 1 can (14 ounces / 414ml) sweetened condensed milk
- 1 cup (240ml) heavy cream

For the Topping (Optional):

- Whipped cream
- Maraschino cherries or fresh fruit for garnish

Instructions:

1. Preheat Oven: Preheat your oven to 350°F (175°C). Grease and flour a 9x13-inch baking pan.
2. Make Cake:
    - In a mixing bowl, sift together the all-purpose flour, baking powder, and salt. Set aside.

- In a separate bowl, beat the egg whites with an electric mixer on high speed until soft peaks form. Gradually add 1/2 cup of granulated sugar and continue to beat until stiff peaks form.
- In another bowl, beat the egg yolks with the remaining 1/2 cup of granulated sugar until pale and fluffy. Stir in the whole milk and vanilla extract until well combined.
- Gently fold the beaten egg whites into the egg yolk mixture until just combined.
- Gradually fold in the dry ingredients until the batter is smooth and well combined.
- Pour the batter into the prepared baking pan and spread it out evenly.
3. Bake Cake: Bake in the preheated oven for 25-30 minutes, or until a toothpick inserted into the center comes out clean and the top is golden brown.
4. Prepare Three Milks Mixture:
    - In a mixing bowl, whisk together the evaporated milk, sweetened condensed milk, and heavy cream until well combined.
5. Soak Cake: Once the cake is baked and still warm, use a fork or skewer to poke holes all over the surface of the cake. Be sure to poke all the way to the bottom of the cake.
    - Slowly pour the three milks mixture over the warm cake, making sure to cover the entire surface evenly. Allow the cake to absorb the mixture for at least 30 minutes, or until all the liquid is absorbed.
6. Chill: Cover the soaked cake with plastic wrap and refrigerate for at least 2 hours, or preferably overnight, to allow the flavors to meld and the cake to set.
7. Serve: Once chilled, slice the tres leches cake into squares and serve chilled. Optionally, top each slice with whipped cream and garnish with maraschino cherries or fresh fruit.
8. Enjoy: Enjoy this moist and decadent Latin American dessert, with its rich and creamy texture and sweet milk flavor!

Tres leches cake is best enjoyed chilled and can be stored covered in the refrigerator for up to 3 days. Serve it as a refreshing treat on a hot day or as a delightful dessert for any occasion!

Strudel (Austria)

Ingredients:

For the Dough:

- 2 cups (250g) all-purpose flour
- Pinch of salt
- 2 tablespoons vegetable oil
- 3/4 cup (180ml) lukewarm water
- 2 tablespoons melted butter, for brushing

For the Filling:

- 4 large apples (such as Granny Smith), peeled, cored, and thinly sliced
- 1/2 cup (100g) granulated sugar
- 1 teaspoon ground cinnamon
- 1/2 cup (50g) breadcrumbs
- 1/2 cup (60g) chopped walnuts or almonds
- Zest of 1 lemon
- 2 tablespoons lemon juice
- 1/4 cup (60ml) melted butter, for brushing

For Garnish:

- Powdered sugar, for dusting
- Whipped cream or vanilla ice cream (optional, for serving)

Instructions:

1. Prepare Dough:
    - In a large mixing bowl, combine the all-purpose flour and a pinch of salt. Make a well in the center and add the vegetable oil and lukewarm water. Mix until a dough forms.

- Knead the dough on a floured surface until it becomes smooth and elastic, about 5-7 minutes. Shape the dough into a ball and brush it lightly with melted butter. Cover with a clean kitchen towel and let it rest for 30 minutes.

2. Prepare Filling:
   - In a mixing bowl, toss together the thinly sliced apples, granulated sugar, ground cinnamon, breadcrumbs, chopped nuts, lemon zest, and lemon juice until well combined. Set aside.

3. Roll Out Dough:
   - Preheat your oven to 375°F (190°C). Line a baking sheet with parchment paper.
   - On a floured surface, roll out the rested dough into a large rectangle, about 14x18 inches in size. The dough should be thin and almost translucent.

4. Fill and Roll Strudel:
   - Brush the rolled-out dough with melted butter, leaving a border around the edges.
   - Spread the apple filling evenly over the buttered dough, leaving a border around the edges.
   - Starting from one of the long edges, carefully roll the dough into a tight cylinder, tucking in the edges as you roll.

5. Bake Strudel:
   - Carefully transfer the rolled strudel onto the prepared baking sheet, seam side down.
   - Brush the top of the strudel with melted butter.
   - Using a sharp knife, make a few diagonal slits on the top of the strudel to allow steam to escape during baking.
   - Bake in the preheated oven for 35-40 minutes, or until the strudel is golden brown and the apples are tender.

6. Serve:
   - Remove the strudel from the oven and let it cool slightly on the baking sheet.
   - Dust the warm strudel with powdered sugar.
   - Slice the apple strudel into portions and serve warm, optionally with whipped cream or vanilla ice cream on the side.

7. Enjoy:
   - Enjoy the delicious aroma and flavor of freshly baked apple strudel, a classic Austrian pastry!

Apple strudel is best enjoyed warm on the day it is baked, but any leftovers can be stored covered in the refrigerator for up to 2 days. Reheat gently in the oven before serving, if desired. Serve this delightful dessert as a treat for family gatherings or special occasions!

Galette (France)

Ingredients:

For the Dough:

- 1 1/4 cups (160g) all-purpose flour
- 1/4 teaspoon salt
- 1/2 cup (115g) unsalted butter, cold and cubed
- 3-4 tablespoons ice water

For the Filling:

- 3-4 cups (about 450-600g) fresh fruit (such as berries, sliced peaches, apples, or pears)
- 1/4 cup (50g) granulated sugar, plus extra for sprinkling
- 1 tablespoon cornstarch or flour
- 1 tablespoon lemon juice
- Zest of 1 lemon (optional)
- 1 egg, beaten (for egg wash)

For Garnish:

- Powdered sugar (optional)
- Vanilla ice cream or whipped cream (optional, for serving)

Instructions:

1. Prepare Dough:
    - In a large mixing bowl, whisk together the all-purpose flour and salt.
    - Add the cold, cubed unsalted butter to the flour mixture. Using a pastry cutter or your fingers, work the butter into the flour until the mixture resembles coarse crumbs with some pea-sized pieces of butter remaining.

- Gradually add the ice water, 1 tablespoon at a time, mixing with a fork, until the dough comes together. Be careful not to overwork the dough. It should hold together when pinched.
    - Shape the dough into a disc, wrap it in plastic wrap, and refrigerate for at least 30 minutes to chill.
2. Preheat Oven: Preheat your oven to 375°F (190°C). Line a baking sheet with parchment paper.
3. Prepare Filling:
    - In a mixing bowl, combine the fresh fruit, granulated sugar, cornstarch or flour, lemon juice, and lemon zest (if using). Toss until the fruit is evenly coated with the sugar mixture.
4. Roll Out Dough:
    - On a lightly floured surface, roll out the chilled dough into a rough circle, about 12-14 inches in diameter and 1/8 inch thick. It doesn't need to be perfectly round.
5. Assemble Galette:
    - Transfer the rolled-out dough to the prepared baking sheet.
    - Arrange the fruit filling in the center of the dough, leaving about 2 inches of dough around the edges.
    - Gently fold the edges of the dough over the fruit filling, pleating as you go, to create a rustic border. Press gently to seal any cracks in the dough.
    - Brush the edges of the dough with the beaten egg, then sprinkle with granulated sugar.
6. Bake Galette:
    - Bake in the preheated oven for 30-35 minutes, or until the crust is golden brown and the fruit is bubbling.
7. Cool and Serve:
    - Remove the galette from the oven and let it cool slightly on the baking sheet.
    - Optional: Dust the warm galette with powdered sugar before serving.
    - Slice the galette into portions and serve warm or at room temperature, optionally with vanilla ice cream or whipped cream on the side.
8. Enjoy:
    - Enjoy the delicious simplicity of this French galette, with its buttery crust and flavorful fruit filling!

Galette is best enjoyed fresh on the day it is baked, but any leftovers can be stored covered at room temperature for up to 2 days. Reheat gently in the oven before serving, if desired. Serve this delightful dessert as a perfect ending to a meal or enjoy it as a sweet treat any time of day!

Trifle (United Kingdom)

Ingredients:

For the Cake Layer:

- 1 store-bought sponge cake or pound cake, cut into cubes (or homemade if preferred)
- 1/4 cup (60ml) sherry or fruit juice (such as orange juice)

For the Custard Layer:

- 2 cups (480ml) whole milk
- 1/2 cup (100g) granulated sugar
- 4 large egg yolks
- 2 tablespoons cornstarch
- 1 teaspoon vanilla extract

For the Fruit Layer:

- 2 cups (about 300g) mixed fresh berries (such as strawberries, raspberries, and blueberries), sliced if large
- 1-2 bananas, sliced
- 1 cup (240ml) fruit jam or preserves (optional)

For the Whipped Cream Layer:

- 1 1/2 cups (360ml) heavy cream
- 2 tablespoons powdered sugar
- 1 teaspoon vanilla extract

For Garnish:

- Fresh berries
- Mint leaves
- Shaved chocolate or cocoa powder

Instructions:

1. Prepare Cake Layer:
   - Arrange the sponge cake or pound cake cubes in the bottom of a trifle dish or large glass bowl. Drizzle the sherry or fruit juice over the cake cubes to moisten them. Set aside.
2. Prepare Custard Layer:
   - In a saucepan, heat the whole milk over medium heat until it just begins to simmer. Remove from heat.
   - In a mixing bowl, whisk together the granulated sugar, egg yolks, and cornstarch until well combined and slightly pale in color.
   - Slowly pour the warm milk into the egg yolk mixture, whisking constantly to temper the eggs.
   - Return the mixture to the saucepan and cook over medium-low heat, stirring constantly, until the custard thickens and coats the back of a spoon. This may take about 5-7 minutes.
   - Remove from heat and stir in the vanilla extract. Let the custard cool slightly.
3. Assemble Trifle:
   - Pour the slightly cooled custard over the cake cubes in the trifle dish, spreading it out evenly.
4. Add Fruit Layer:
   - Arrange the mixed fresh berries and sliced bananas over the custard layer. If using, spread the fruit jam or preserves over the fruit layer.
5. Prepare Whipped Cream Layer:
   - In a mixing bowl, beat the heavy cream, powdered sugar, and vanilla extract together until soft peaks form.
6. Top with Whipped Cream:
   - Spread the whipped cream over the fruit layer, covering it completely.
7. Garnish:
   - Garnish the top of the trifle with fresh berries, mint leaves, and shaved chocolate or a dusting of cocoa powder.
8. Chill and Serve:

- Cover the trifle with plastic wrap and refrigerate for at least 2 hours, or preferably overnight, to allow the flavors to meld and the layers to set.
- Serve chilled and enjoy the layers of cake, custard, fruit, and whipped cream in every spoonful!

Trifle is a classic British dessert that is perfect for special occasions or gatherings. It can be prepared ahead of time and assembled just before serving. Enjoy the creamy, fruity goodness of this delightful dessert!

Poffertjes (Netherlands)

Ingredients:

- 1 cup (125g) all-purpose flour
- 1 teaspoon active dry yeast
- 1 tablespoon granulated sugar
- 1/2 cup (120ml) lukewarm milk
- 1 large egg
- Pinch of salt
- Butter or oil, for greasing the pan
- Powdered sugar, for dusting
- Optional toppings: melted butter, maple syrup, Nutella, whipped cream, fresh berries

Instructions:

1. Prepare Batter:
    - In a small bowl, combine the active dry yeast, granulated sugar, and lukewarm milk. Let it sit for about 5-10 minutes, or until foamy.
2. Mix Batter:
    - In a large mixing bowl, whisk together the flour and salt. Make a well in the center and pour in the yeast mixture. Crack in the egg.
    - Using a whisk or spoon, gradually incorporate the flour into the wet ingredients until you have a smooth batter. The batter should be thick but pourable. If it's too thick, you can add a little more milk.
3. Rest Batter:
    - Cover the bowl with plastic wrap or a clean kitchen towel and let the batter rest in a warm place for about 30-45 minutes. During this time, the batter will rise and become slightly bubbly.
4. Preheat Poffertjes Pan:
    - Heat a poffertjes pan or aebleskiver pan over medium-low heat. Lightly grease each indentation with butter or oil.
5. Cook Poffertjes:
    - Once the pan is hot, fill each indentation about three-quarters full with batter using a spoon or a piping bag. Cook the poffertjes for 2-3 minutes,

or until small bubbles form on the surface and the bottoms are golden brown.
    - Use a skewer or fork to carefully flip each poffertje over and cook for an additional 1-2 minutes, or until the other side is golden brown and cooked through.
6. Serve:
    - Transfer the cooked poffertjes to a serving plate. Repeat the cooking process with the remaining batter, greasing the pan as needed.
    - Dust the warm poffertjes with powdered sugar.
    - Serve immediately with your choice of toppings, such as melted butter, maple syrup, Nutella, whipped cream, or fresh berries.
7. Enjoy:
    - Enjoy these fluffy and delicious Dutch mini pancakes as a delightful snack or dessert!

Poffertjes are best served warm and freshly cooked. They can be enjoyed as a treat on their own or as part of a larger breakfast or brunch spread. Customize them with your favorite toppings for a truly indulgent experience!

Loukoumades (Greece)

Ingredients:

For the Dough:

- 2 cups (250g) all-purpose flour
- 1 teaspoon instant yeast
- 1/2 teaspoon salt
- 1 tablespoon granulated sugar
- 1 1/4 cups (300ml) lukewarm water

For Frying:

- Vegetable oil, for frying

For Syrup:

- 1 cup (200g) granulated sugar
- 1/2 cup (120ml) water
- 1 tablespoon honey
- 1 cinnamon stick (optional)
- Zest of 1 lemon or orange (optional)

Optional Toppings:

- Ground cinnamon
- Chopped nuts (such as walnuts or almonds)
- Drizzle of honey or chocolate syrup

Instructions:

1. Prepare Dough:

- In a large mixing bowl, combine the all-purpose flour, instant yeast, salt, and granulated sugar. Gradually add the lukewarm water while stirring, until a smooth batter forms. Cover the bowl with plastic wrap or a clean kitchen towel and let the dough rest in a warm place for about 1-2 hours, or until it doubles in size.

2. Make Syrup:
   - In a saucepan, combine the granulated sugar, water, honey, and cinnamon stick (if using). Bring the mixture to a boil over medium heat, stirring occasionally until the sugar is completely dissolved. Simmer for a few minutes until slightly thickened. Remove from heat and stir in the lemon or orange zest (if using). Set aside to cool.

3. Fry Loukoumades:
   - Heat vegetable oil in a deep fryer or a deep, heavy-bottomed pot to 350°F (175°C).
   - Using a spoon or a small ice cream scoop, carefully drop spoonfuls of the dough into the hot oil, frying in batches to avoid overcrowding. Fry until golden brown and puffed, about 2-3 minutes, flipping them occasionally for even cooking.

4. Drain and Coat:
   - Remove the fried loukoumades from the oil using a slotted spoon and transfer them to a plate lined with paper towels to drain excess oil.
   - While still warm, dip the loukoumades into the cooled syrup, coating them evenly. Let them soak in the syrup for a few seconds, then transfer them to a serving platter.

5. Serve:
   - Arrange the loukoumades on a serving platter and sprinkle them with ground cinnamon and chopped nuts, if desired.
   - Drizzle with additional honey or chocolate syrup for extra sweetness, if desired.
   - Serve the loukoumades warm and enjoy their deliciously crispy exterior and soft, fluffy interior soaked in fragrant syrup!

Loukoumades are best served fresh and warm. They are a popular Greek dessert enjoyed on special occasions and during festive celebrations. Share these delightful bite-sized treats with family and friends for a taste of Greek sweetness!

Cannoli Cake (Italy)

Ingredients:

For the Cake:

- 2 cups (250g) all-purpose flour
- 2 teaspoons baking powder
- 1/2 teaspoon baking soda
- 1/2 teaspoon salt
- 1/2 cup (115g) unsalted butter, softened
- 1 cup (200g) granulated sugar
- 3 large eggs
- 1 teaspoon vanilla extract
- 1 cup (240ml) buttermilk

For the Cannoli Filling:

- 1 1/2 cups (360g) ricotta cheese
- 1/2 cup (60g) powdered sugar
- 1 teaspoon vanilla extract
- Zest of 1 orange
- 1/4 cup (30g) mini chocolate chips
- 1/4 cup (30g) chopped pistachios

For the Frosting:

- 1 1/2 cups (360ml) heavy cream
- 1/2 cup (60g) powdered sugar
- 1 teaspoon vanilla extract

For Garnish:

- Mini chocolate chips

- Chopped pistachios
- Cannoli shells, broken into pieces

Instructions:

1. Preheat Oven: Preheat your oven to 350°F (175°C). Grease and flour two 9-inch round cake pans.
2. Make Cake:
   - In a mixing bowl, sift together the all-purpose flour, baking powder, baking soda, and salt. Set aside.
   - In another bowl, cream together the softened butter and granulated sugar until light and fluffy. Add the eggs one at a time, beating well after each addition. Stir in the vanilla extract.
   - Gradually add the dry ingredients to the wet ingredients, alternating with the buttermilk, and mix until well combined.
   - Divide the cake batter evenly between the prepared cake pans and spread it out evenly.
   - Bake in the preheated oven for 25-30 minutes, or until a toothpick inserted into the center comes out clean.
   - Remove from the oven and let the cakes cool in the pans for 10 minutes before transferring them to wire racks to cool completely.
3. Make Cannoli Filling:
   - In a mixing bowl, combine the ricotta cheese, powdered sugar, vanilla extract, and orange zest until smooth and creamy.
   - Fold in the mini chocolate chips and chopped pistachios until evenly distributed.
4. Make Frosting:
   - In a separate mixing bowl, beat the heavy cream, powdered sugar, and vanilla extract until stiff peaks form.
5. Assemble Cake:
   - Place one cooled cake layer on a serving platter. Spread a layer of the cannoli filling evenly over the top.
   - Place the second cake layer on top and gently press down.
   - Frost the top and sides of the cake with the whipped cream frosting.
6. Garnish:
   - Garnish the top of the cake with mini chocolate chips, chopped pistachios, and broken pieces of cannoli shells.
7. Chill and Serve:

- Refrigerate the cannoli cake for at least 1 hour before serving to allow the flavors to meld and the frosting to set.
- Slice and serve the delicious cannoli cake as a decadent dessert for any occasion!

This cannoli cake combines the flavors of traditional Italian cannoli with the lightness of cake and whipped cream frosting. It's sure to be a hit with cannoli lovers and dessert enthusiasts alike! Enjoy the rich and creamy goodness of this delightful dessert.

Brigadeiro (Brazil)

Ingredients:

- 1 can (14 ounces / 397g) sweetened condensed milk
- 2 tablespoons unsweetened cocoa powder
- 1 tablespoon unsalted butter, plus extra for greasing
- Chocolate sprinkles or finely chopped nuts, for coating (optional)

Instructions:

1. Prepare Pan:
    - Lightly grease a plate or baking sheet with butter. This will prevent the brigadeiro mixture from sticking.
2. Make Brigadeiro Mixture:
    - In a non-stick saucepan, combine the sweetened condensed milk, unsweetened cocoa powder, and unsalted butter.
    - Cook the mixture over medium heat, stirring constantly with a wooden spoon or silicone spatula, until it thickens and pulls away from the sides of the pan. This will take about 10-15 minutes. The brigadeiro mixture should have a fudgy consistency.
3. Cool Mixture:
    - Transfer the brigadeiro mixture to the greased plate or baking sheet. Let it cool to room temperature. This will make it easier to handle and shape.
4. Shape Brigadeiros:
    - Once the mixture has cooled, lightly grease your hands with butter to prevent sticking. Take small portions of the brigadeiro mixture and roll them into small balls, about 1-inch in diameter, between your palms.
5. Coat Brigadeiros (Optional):
    - If desired, roll the brigadeiro balls in chocolate sprinkles or finely chopped nuts to coat them evenly. This adds texture and extra flavor to the brigadeiros.
6. Serve:
    - Arrange the brigadeiros on a serving platter or in small paper cups.
    - Enjoy these delicious Brazilian treats as a sweet snack or dessert!

Brigadeiros are a popular Brazilian confection enjoyed at birthday parties, celebrations, and gatherings. They are simple to make and can be customized with different coatings or toppings according to your preference. Enjoy the rich and chocolaty flavor of these delightful treats!

Sacher Torte (Austria)

Ingredients:

For the Cake:

- 7 ounces (200g) dark chocolate (at least 60% cocoa solids), chopped
- 7 tablespoons (100g) unsalted butter, softened
- 3/4 cup (150g) granulated sugar
- 6 large eggs, separated
- 1 teaspoon vanilla extract
- 1 cup (120g) all-purpose flour
- 1/2 cup (50g) ground almonds or almond flour
- Pinch of salt

For the Apricot Jam Filling:

- 3/4 cup (200g) apricot jam

For the Chocolate Glaze:

- 7 ounces (200g) dark chocolate (at least 60% cocoa solids), chopped
- 1/2 cup (120ml) heavy cream
- 2 tablespoons unsalted butter

For Garnish:

- Whipped cream
- Whole or sliced almonds

Instructions:

1. Preheat Oven and Prepare Pan:

- Preheat your oven to 350°F (175°C). Grease a 9-inch (23cm) round cake pan and line the bottom with parchment paper.
2. Melt Chocolate:
    - In a heatproof bowl set over a pot of simmering water, melt the chopped dark chocolate, stirring occasionally until smooth. Remove from heat and let it cool slightly.
3. Make Cake Batter:
    - In a mixing bowl, cream together the softened butter and granulated sugar until light and fluffy.
    - Add the egg yolks one at a time, beating well after each addition. Stir in the vanilla extract.
    - Gradually fold in the melted chocolate until well combined.
    - In a separate bowl, whisk together the all-purpose flour, ground almonds, and salt.
    - Gently fold the flour mixture into the chocolate mixture until just combined.
4. Whip Egg Whites:
    - In a clean mixing bowl, using clean beaters, beat the egg whites until stiff peaks form.
5. Fold in Egg Whites:
    - Carefully fold the beaten egg whites into the chocolate batter until no streaks remain. Be gentle to maintain the airiness of the batter.
6. Bake Cake:
    - Pour the batter into the prepared cake pan and smooth the top with a spatula.
    - Bake in the preheated oven for 35-40 minutes, or until a toothpick inserted into the center comes out clean.
    - Remove from the oven and let the cake cool in the pan for 10 minutes before transferring it to a wire rack to cool completely.
7. Prepare Apricot Jam Filling:
    - In a small saucepan, heat the apricot jam over low heat until it becomes smooth and spreadable. Set aside to cool slightly.
8. Assemble Cake:
    - Once the cake has cooled completely, carefully slice it in half horizontally to create two layers.
    - Spread a generous layer of apricot jam over the bottom half of the cake, then place the other half on top.
9. Make Chocolate Glaze:

- In a heatproof bowl set over a pot of simmering water, melt the chopped dark chocolate and heavy cream, stirring until smooth. Remove from heat and stir in the unsalted butter until fully incorporated.
10. Glaze Cake:
    - Pour the chocolate glaze over the top of the cake, allowing it to drip down the sides. Use a spatula to spread the glaze evenly, if needed.
11. Chill Cake:
    - Transfer the cake to the refrigerator and chill for at least 1 hour, or until the glaze is set.
12. Garnish and Serve:
    - Before serving, garnish the Sacher Torte with whipped cream and whole or sliced almonds.
    - Slice and serve this classic Austrian dessert to enjoy its rich chocolate flavor and delightful apricot filling!

Sacher Torte is best served chilled and can be stored covered in the refrigerator for up to 3 days. Enjoy this decadent treat with friends and family on special occasions or whenever you're craving a taste of Austrian indulgence!

Mille-Feuille (France)

Ingredients:

For the Puff Pastry:

- 1 sheet of store-bought puff pastry (about 9x9 inches or 23x23 cm), thawed if frozen

For the Pastry Cream:

- 1 1/2 cups (360ml) whole milk
- 1/2 cup (100g) granulated sugar
- 4 large egg yolks
- 1/4 cup (30g) cornstarch
- 1 teaspoon vanilla extract

For Assembly:

- Powdered sugar, for dusting
- Optional: Fresh berries, sliced fruits, or chocolate drizzle for garnish

Instructions:

1. Preheat Oven and Prepare Puff Pastry:
    - Preheat your oven to 400°F (200°C). Line a baking sheet with parchment paper.
    - Place the thawed puff pastry sheet on the prepared baking sheet. Prick the pastry all over with a fork to prevent it from puffing up too much during baking.
2. Bake Puff Pastry:
    - Bake the puff pastry in the preheated oven for 15-20 minutes, or until golden brown and puffed up. Keep an eye on it to prevent burning. Once

baked, remove from the oven and let it cool completely on the baking sheet.
3. Make Pastry Cream:
    - In a saucepan, heat the whole milk over medium heat until it just begins to simmer. Remove from heat.
    - In a mixing bowl, whisk together the granulated sugar, egg yolks, and cornstarch until smooth and creamy.
    - Gradually pour the warm milk into the egg mixture, whisking constantly to temper the eggs.
    - Return the mixture to the saucepan and cook over medium-low heat, stirring constantly, until the pastry cream thickens and coats the back of a spoon. This may take about 5-7 minutes.
    - Remove from heat and stir in the vanilla extract. Let the pastry cream cool to room temperature, then cover with plastic wrap, pressing it directly onto the surface of the cream to prevent a skin from forming. Refrigerate until chilled and firm.
4. Assemble Mille-Feuille:
    - Once the puff pastry and pastry cream are completely cooled, carefully cut the baked puff pastry into three equal-sized rectangles.
    - Place one rectangle of puff pastry on a serving platter or plate. Spread a layer of pastry cream evenly over the pastry.
    - Place another rectangle of puff pastry on top of the pastry cream layer and press down gently.
    - Repeat the process by spreading another layer of pastry cream over the second pastry layer, then topping it with the third rectangle of puff pastry.
    - Dust the top of the mille-feuille with powdered sugar.
5. Garnish and Serve:
    - Garnish the top of the mille-feuille with fresh berries, sliced fruits, or a drizzle of chocolate, if desired.
    - Slice the mille-feuille into portions using a sharp knife and serve immediately.
6. Enjoy:
    - Enjoy this classic French dessert with its layers of flaky puff pastry and creamy pastry cream, a perfect balance of textures and flavors!

Mille-feuille is best enjoyed fresh on the day it is assembled, as the puff pastry may soften over time. Serve this elegant dessert as a delightful treat for special occasions or as a sweet ending to any meal!

Sticky Toffee Pudding (United Kingdom)

Ingredients:

For the Cake:

- 1 cup (200g) pitted dates, chopped
- 1 cup (240ml) boiling water
- 1 teaspoon baking soda
- 1 3/4 cups (220g) all-purpose flour
- 1 teaspoon baking powder
- 1/2 teaspoon salt
- 1/2 cup (115g) unsalted butter, softened
- 1 cup (200g) granulated sugar
- 2 large eggs
- 1 teaspoon vanilla extract

For the Toffee Sauce:

- 1 cup (200g) packed brown sugar
- 1/2 cup (115g) unsalted butter
- 3/4 cup (180ml) heavy cream
- Pinch of salt

For Serving:

- Vanilla ice cream or whipped cream

Instructions:

1. Prepare Dates:
    - In a heatproof bowl, place the chopped dates and sprinkle baking soda over them. Pour boiling water over the dates and let them soak for about 15-20 minutes.

2. **Preheat Oven and Prepare Pan:**
   - Preheat your oven to 350°F (175°C). Grease a 9x9-inch (23x23cm) square baking pan or a similar-sized dish.
3. **Make Cake Batter:**
   - In a mixing bowl, whisk together the all-purpose flour, baking powder, and salt. Set aside.
   - In another bowl, cream together the softened butter and granulated sugar until light and fluffy. Beat in the eggs, one at a time, followed by the vanilla extract.
   - Gradually add the flour mixture to the wet ingredients, mixing until just combined.
   - Fold in the soaked dates and any remaining liquid until evenly distributed.
4. **Bake Cake:**
   - Pour the cake batter into the prepared baking pan, spreading it out evenly.
   - Bake in the preheated oven for 30-35 minutes, or until a toothpick inserted into the center comes out clean.
5. **Make Toffee Sauce:**
   - While the cake is baking, prepare the toffee sauce. In a saucepan, combine the brown sugar, unsalted butter, heavy cream, and a pinch of salt.
   - Cook over medium heat, stirring constantly, until the mixture comes to a gentle boil and thickens slightly, about 5-7 minutes. Remove from heat and set aside.
6. **Serve:**
   - Once the cake is baked, remove it from the oven and let it cool slightly in the pan for about 10 minutes.
   - Using a skewer or fork, poke holes all over the top of the warm cake.
   - Pour about half of the warm toffee sauce evenly over the warm cake, allowing it to soak in.
   - Slice the sticky toffee pudding and serve warm, drizzled with extra toffee sauce and topped with vanilla ice cream or whipped cream.
7. **Enjoy:**
   - Enjoy this indulgent British dessert with its moist and flavorful cake, soaked in rich toffee sauce, served warm with a creamy accompaniment!

Sticky toffee pudding is best enjoyed warm, but any leftovers can be stored covered in the refrigerator for up to 3 days. Reheat gently in the microwave or oven before serving. It's a perfect comfort dessert for cold evenings or as a sweet treat any time of year!

Mochi Ice Cream (Japan)

Ingredients:

For the Mochi Dough:

- 1 cup (150g) glutinous rice flour (also known as sweet rice flour or mochiko)
- 1/4 cup (50g) granulated sugar
- 1 cup (240ml) water
- Potato starch or cornstarch, for dusting

For Assembly:

- Your choice of ice cream flavors, slightly softened (common flavors include vanilla, chocolate, green tea, strawberry, mango, etc.)
- Additional toppings or coatings, such as matcha powder, cocoa powder, chopped nuts, or sprinkles (optional)

Instructions:

1. Prepare Mochi Dough:
    - In a microwave-safe bowl, whisk together the glutinous rice flour and granulated sugar until well combined.
    - Gradually add the water to the flour mixture, stirring until smooth and free of lumps.
2. Microwave Mochi Dough:
    - Cover the bowl loosely with plastic wrap or a microwave-safe lid.
    - Microwave the mochi dough mixture on high for 1 minute. Carefully remove from the microwave and stir well.
3. Continue Cooking Mochi Dough:
    - Re-cover the bowl and microwave for an additional 1 minute. Stir again.
4. Form Mochi Balls:
    - The dough should be sticky and stretchy. If it's too dry, add a teaspoon of water at a time until you achieve the desired consistency.
    - Dust a clean surface with potato starch or cornstarch to prevent sticking.

- While the dough is still warm, scoop out small portions and flatten them into discs using your hands or a rolling pin.
5. Wrap Ice Cream:
   - Place a small scoop of slightly softened ice cream in the center of each mochi disc.
   - Carefully fold the edges of the mochi around the ice cream, pinching to seal and form a ball.
6. Freeze Mochi Ice Cream:
   - Place the mochi ice cream balls on a baking sheet lined with parchment paper.
   - Freeze the mochi ice cream balls for at least 2 hours, or until firm.
7. Optional: Coat or Garnish:
   - If desired, roll the frozen mochi ice cream balls in additional toppings or coatings, such as matcha powder, cocoa powder, chopped nuts, or sprinkles.
8. Serve and Enjoy:
   - Serve the mochi ice cream balls immediately as a delicious and refreshing treat!
   - Alternatively, store any leftovers in an airtight container in the freezer for up to a few weeks.

Mochi ice cream is a delightful Japanese dessert that combines the chewy texture of mochi with the cold creaminess of ice cream. Experiment with different ice cream flavors and coatings to create your own unique variations!

Kulfi (India)

Ingredients:

- 4 cups (1 liter) full-fat milk
- 1/2 cup (100g) sugar (adjust to taste)
- 1/2 cup (75g) mixed nuts (such as almonds, cashews, pistachios), finely chopped
- 1/2 teaspoon cardamom powder
- 1 tablespoon cornstarch (optional)
- Saffron strands (optional)
- Kulfi molds or small disposable cups
- Ice cream sticks or popsicle sticks

Instructions:

1. Prepare Milk Mixture:
    - In a heavy-bottomed saucepan, bring the full-fat milk to a gentle boil over medium heat, stirring occasionally to prevent it from sticking to the bottom of the pan.
2. Reduce Heat and Simmer:
    - Once the milk comes to a boil, reduce the heat to low and let it simmer for about 30-40 minutes, stirring occasionally. The milk will gradually reduce and thicken.
3. Add Sugar and Flavorings:
    - Add the sugar to the simmering milk and stir until it dissolves completely.
    - Stir in the cardamom powder and saffron strands (if using) for flavor. You can also add a tablespoon of cornstarch mixed with water at this point to help thicken the kulfi further, if desired.
4. Cool Mixture:
    - Let the milk mixture cool to room temperature. Stir in the finely chopped mixed nuts.
5. Fill Molds:
    - Pour the cooled milk mixture into kulfi molds or small disposable cups, filling them about 3/4 full. Insert an ice cream stick or popsicle stick into the center of each mold.
6. Freeze Kulfi:

- Place the filled molds in the freezer and let them freeze for at least 6-8 hours, or until completely set.
7. Serve Kulfi:
    - Once the kulfi is fully frozen, remove the molds from the freezer.
    - To unmold the kulfi, briefly dip the bottom of each mold in warm water for a few seconds to loosen the kulfi.
    - Gently pull on the ice cream sticks to remove the kulfi from the molds.
    - Serve the delicious homemade kulfi immediately as a refreshing frozen dessert!

Kulfi is a popular Indian frozen dessert enjoyed during hot summer days or as a sweet treat after a meal. It's creamy, rich, and flavored with cardamom and nuts, making it irresistible to anyone with a sweet tooth! Experiment with different variations by adding flavors such as rose water, saffron, or mango pulp for a unique twist on this classic Indian dessert.

Pavê de Chocolate (Brazil)

Ingredientes:

Para o Creme de Chocolate:

- 2 latas (800g) de leite condensado
- 2 colheres de sopa (30g) de manteiga sem sal
- 6 colheres de sopa (40g) de cacau em pó
- 1 xícara (240ml) de leite
- 2 gemas de ovo
- 2 colheres de sopa (15g) de amido de milho (maisena)
- 200g de chocolate meio amargo, picado

Para Montar o Pavê:

- 1 pacote (200g) de biscoito maisena ou champagne
- 1 xícara (240ml) de leite
- Chocolate em raspas ou cacau em pó para decorar

Instruções:

1. Preparar o Creme de Chocolate:
    - Em uma panela, misture o leite condensado, a manteiga, o cacau em pó, o leite, as gemas de ovo e o amido de milho.
    - Cozinhe em fogo médio, mexendo constantemente, até que a mistura engrosse e comece a soltar do fundo da panela, formando um creme.
    - Retire do fogo e acrescente o chocolate meio amargo picado, mexendo até que derreta completamente e se incorpore ao creme. Reserve.
2. Montar o Pavê:
    - Em um prato de servir ou em uma travessa, faça uma camada de biscoitos maisena ou champagne previamente molhados no leite.
    - Cubra os biscoitos com uma camada do creme de chocolate preparado anteriormente.

- Repita as camadas alternando entre biscoitos e creme até utilizar todos os ingredientes, finalizando com uma camada de creme.
3. Decorar e Refrigerar:
    - Decore a última camada de creme com raspas de chocolate ou polvilhe cacau em pó por cima.
    - Cubra o pavê com filme plástico e leve à geladeira por pelo menos 4 horas, ou até que esteja firme.
4. Servir:
    - Retire o pavê da geladeira e corte em pedaços para servir.
    - Sirva o delicioso pavê de chocolate gelado como sobremesa em ocasiões especiais ou sempre que desejar um doce irresistível!

O pavê de chocolate é uma sobremesa clássica e muito apreciada no Brasil, perfeita para satisfazer os amantes de chocolate. Com suas camadas cremosas e sabor intenso de cacau, é uma opção indulgente para qualquer ocasião.

Eclairs (France)

Ingredients:

For the Choux Pastry:

- 1/2 cup (120ml) water
- 1/2 cup (120ml) whole milk
- 1/2 cup (115g) unsalted butter, cut into cubes
- 1 tablespoon granulated sugar
- 1/4 teaspoon salt
- 1 cup (125g) all-purpose flour
- 4 large eggs

For the Pastry Cream Filling:

- 1 1/4 cups (300ml) whole milk
- 4 large egg yolks
- 1/4 cup (50g) granulated sugar
- 2 tablespoons cornstarch
- 1 teaspoon vanilla extract

For the Chocolate Glaze:

- 4 ounces (115g) semisweet chocolate, chopped
- 1/2 cup (120ml) heavy cream
- 1 tablespoon unsalted butter

Instructions:

1. Prepare Choux Pastry:
    - Preheat your oven to 400°F (200°C). Line a baking sheet with parchment paper.
    - In a medium saucepan, combine water, milk, butter, sugar, and salt. Bring to a boil over medium heat.

- Once boiling, reduce the heat to low and add the flour all at once. Stir vigorously with a wooden spoon until the mixture forms a ball and pulls away from the sides of the pan.
- Transfer the dough to a mixing bowl and let it cool slightly, about 5 minutes.
- Add the eggs one at a time, beating well after each addition, until the dough is smooth and glossy.

2. Pipe and Bake Éclairs:
   - Transfer the choux pastry dough to a piping bag fitted with a large round tip.
   - Pipe 4-inch (10cm) long strips onto the prepared baking sheet, spacing them a few inches apart.
   - Bake in the preheated oven for 15 minutes, then reduce the oven temperature to 350°F (180°C) and continue baking for another 20-25 minutes, or until golden brown and puffed.
   - Remove from the oven and let the éclairs cool completely on a wire rack.

3. Prepare Pastry Cream Filling:
   - In a saucepan, heat the milk over medium heat until it just begins to simmer.
   - In a mixing bowl, whisk together the egg yolks, sugar, and cornstarch until smooth.
   - Gradually pour the hot milk into the egg yolk mixture, whisking constantly to temper the eggs.
   - Return the mixture to the saucepan and cook over medium heat, stirring constantly, until it thickens and coats the back of a spoon.
   - Remove from heat and stir in the vanilla extract. Transfer the pastry cream to a bowl and cover with plastic wrap, pressing it directly onto the surface to prevent a skin from forming. Let it cool completely.

4. Fill Éclairs:
   - Once the éclairs and pastry cream are completely cooled, use a small knife to make a slit along the side of each éclair, creating a pocket for the filling.
   - Transfer the pastry cream to a piping bag fitted with a small round tip. Pipe the cream into each éclair until filled.

5. Prepare Chocolate Glaze:
   - In a heatproof bowl, combine the chopped chocolate, heavy cream, and butter. Microwave in 30-second intervals, stirring between each interval, until the chocolate is melted and the mixture is smooth.

6. Glaze Éclairs:

- Dip the top of each filled éclair into the chocolate glaze, allowing any excess to drip off.
- Place the glazed éclairs on a wire rack set over a baking sheet to catch any drips. Let the glaze set at room temperature for about 10-15 minutes.

7. Serve and Enjoy:
    - Once the glaze is set, serve the delicious homemade éclairs immediately as a delightful treat or dessert!

Éclairs are a classic French pastry enjoyed around the world for their light, airy texture and decadent filling. With their crisp choux pastry shells, creamy pastry cream filling, and rich chocolate glaze, they are sure to impress any dessert lover!

Semla (Sweden)

Ingredients:

For the Buns:

- 3/4 cup (180ml) whole milk
- 2 1/4 teaspoons (1 packet) active dry yeast
- 1/4 cup (50g) granulated sugar
- 1/2 teaspoon salt
- 1 teaspoon ground cardamom
- 1/4 cup (60g) unsalted butter, melted
- 1 large egg
- 3 cups (375g) all-purpose flour, plus extra for dusting

For the Almond Filling:

- 1 cup (100g) almond flour or finely ground almonds
- 1/2 cup (100g) granulated sugar
- 1/2 cup (120ml) whole milk
- 1 teaspoon vanilla extract

For Assembly:

- Powdered sugar, for dusting
- Whipped cream

Instructions:

1. Prepare the Dough:
    - In a small saucepan, heat the milk over low heat until it is warm but not hot to the touch.
    - Transfer the warm milk to a large mixing bowl. Sprinkle the yeast over the milk and let it sit for about 5 minutes until it becomes frothy.

- Add the granulated sugar, salt, ground cardamom, melted butter, and egg to the bowl with the yeast mixture. Stir until well combined.
- Gradually add the flour, stirring until a dough forms.
- Transfer the dough to a floured surface and knead it for about 5-7 minutes, or until it becomes smooth and elastic.
- Place the dough in a lightly greased bowl, cover with a clean kitchen towel, and let it rise in a warm place for about 1 hour, or until doubled in size.

2. Make the Almond Filling:
   - In a mixing bowl, combine the almond flour, granulated sugar, whole milk, and vanilla extract until smooth. Set aside.

3. Shape and Bake the Buns:
   - Preheat your oven to 400°F (200°C). Line a baking sheet with parchment paper.
   - Punch down the risen dough and divide it into 12 equal portions. Shape each portion into a smooth ball and place them on the prepared baking sheet, leaving space between each bun.
   - Cover the buns with a clean kitchen towel and let them rise for an additional 30 minutes.
   - Bake the risen buns in the preheated oven for 12-15 minutes, or until golden brown and cooked through.
   - Remove from the oven and let the buns cool completely on a wire rack.

4. Assemble the Semla:
   - Once the buns are cool, use a sharp knife to cut a small circle from the top of each bun. Set the tops aside.
   - Scoop out some of the inside of each bun to create a hollow space for the filling.
   - Fill each hollowed-out bun with a generous spoonful of the almond filling.
   - Replace the tops of the buns.
   - Dust the tops of the filled buns with powdered sugar.
   - Serve each semla with a dollop of whipped cream on top.

5. Enjoy:
   - Serve these delightful Swedish semla buns as a traditional treat enjoyed during the Lenten season or as a delicious pastry any time of year!

Semla is a classic Swedish pastry typically enjoyed during the Lenten season, although it has become popular year-round in Sweden and beyond. With its light and fluffy bun filled with almond paste and whipped cream, it's a delightful indulgence for pastry lovers everywhere!

Cinnamon Rolls (Sweden)

Ingredients:

For the Dough:

- 1 cup (240ml) whole milk
- 1/4 cup (60g) unsalted butter
- 1/4 cup (50g) granulated sugar
- 2 1/4 teaspoons (1 packet) active dry yeast
- 1/2 teaspoon salt
- 3 1/2 cups (440g) all-purpose flour, plus extra for dusting

For the Filling:

- 1/4 cup (50g) unsalted butter, softened
- 1/2 cup (100g) light brown sugar, packed
- 2 tablespoons ground cinnamon

For the Glaze:

- 1 cup (120g) powdered sugar
- 2-3 tablespoons whole milk
- 1/2 teaspoon vanilla extract

Instructions:

1. Prepare the Dough:
    - In a small saucepan, heat the milk and butter over low heat until the butter is melted. Remove from heat and let it cool until warm but not hot.
    - In a large mixing bowl, combine the warm milk mixture, granulated sugar, and yeast. Let it sit for about 5 minutes until the yeast is foamy.
    - Add the salt and flour to the yeast mixture. Stir until a dough forms.
    - Transfer the dough to a lightly floured surface and knead it for about 5-7 minutes, or until it becomes smooth and elastic.
    - Place the dough in a lightly greased bowl, cover with a clean kitchen towel, and let it rise in a warm place for about 1 hour, or until doubled in size.

2. Prepare the Filling:
   - In a small bowl, mix together the softened butter, light brown sugar, and ground cinnamon until well combined. Set aside.
3. Shape the Rolls:
   - Punch down the risen dough and transfer it to a lightly floured surface.
   - Roll out the dough into a rectangle, about 12x18 inches (30x45cm) in size.
   - Spread the prepared cinnamon filling evenly over the surface of the dough.
   - Starting from one long edge, tightly roll up the dough into a log.
4. Slice and Arrange the Rolls:
   - Using a sharp knife or dental floss, cut the rolled dough into 12 equal-sized slices.
   - Place the slices in a greased baking dish, leaving space between each roll for rising.
5. Let Rise Again:
   - Cover the baking dish with a clean kitchen towel and let the rolls rise for an additional 30 minutes.
6. Bake the Rolls:
   - Preheat your oven to 375°F (190°C).
   - Once the rolls have risen, bake them in the preheated oven for 20-25 minutes, or until golden brown and cooked through.
7. Prepare the Glaze:
   - In a small bowl, whisk together the powdered sugar, milk, and vanilla extract until smooth. Adjust the consistency by adding more milk if needed.
8. Glaze and Serve:
   - Remove the cinnamon rolls from the oven and let them cool slightly.
   - Drizzle the glaze over the warm rolls.
   - Serve the delicious Swedish cinnamon rolls (kanelbullar) warm with a cup of coffee or tea.

Swedish cinnamon rolls, known as kanelbullar, are a beloved treat enjoyed throughout Sweden and beyond. With their soft, fluffy texture and aromatic cinnamon filling, they're perfect for breakfast, brunch, or as a sweet snack any time of day!

Sopapillas (Mexico)

Ingredients:

For the Dough:

- 2 cups (250g) all-purpose flour, plus extra for dusting
- 1 teaspoon baking powder
- 1/2 teaspoon salt
- 2 tablespoons granulated sugar
- 2 tablespoons unsalted butter, melted
- 2/3 cup (160ml) warm water

For Frying:

- Vegetable oil, for frying

For Serving:

- Honey
- Cinnamon sugar (optional)
- Whipped cream or ice cream (optional)

Instructions:

1. Prepare the Dough:
    - In a mixing bowl, whisk together the all-purpose flour, baking powder, salt, and granulated sugar until well combined.
    - Add the melted butter to the dry ingredients and mix until crumbly.
    - Gradually add the warm water, stirring until a dough forms.
    - Turn the dough out onto a lightly floured surface and knead it for a few minutes until smooth.
    - Shape the dough into a ball, cover it with a clean kitchen towel, and let it rest for about 15-20 minutes.

2. Roll and Cut the Dough:
   - After resting, divide the dough into smaller portions for easier handling.
   - On a floured surface, roll out each portion of dough into a thin sheet, about 1/8 inch (3mm) thick.
   - Use a knife or pizza cutter to cut the rolled-out dough into squares or rectangles, about 2-3 inches (5-7.5cm) in size.
3. Fry the Sopapillas:
   - In a deep skillet or frying pan, heat vegetable oil over medium heat until it reaches 350°F (175°C).
   - Carefully add a few pieces of dough to the hot oil, making sure not to overcrowd the pan.
   - Fry the sopapillas for about 1-2 minutes on each side, or until they are puffed up and golden brown.
   - Use a slotted spoon or tongs to transfer the fried sopapillas to a plate lined with paper towels to drain excess oil.
   - Continue frying the remaining dough pieces in batches until all are cooked.
4. Serve:
   - Serve the warm sopapillas immediately with honey drizzled over the top.
   - Optionally, sprinkle cinnamon sugar over the sopapillas for extra flavor.
   - Enjoy the sopapillas as they are, or serve them with a dollop of whipped cream or a scoop of ice cream for a decadent treat!

Sopapillas are a popular Mexican dessert, known for their light and fluffy texture and delightful sweetness. Whether enjoyed on their own or paired with honey, cinnamon sugar, whipped cream, or ice cream, sopapillas are sure to be a hit at any gathering or as a sweet ending to a Mexican-inspired meal!

Bienenstich (Germany)

Ingredients:

For the Dough:

- 2 1/4 cups (280g) all-purpose flour
- 1/4 cup (50g) granulated sugar
- 1 teaspoon salt
- 1 packet (2 1/4 teaspoons) active dry yeast
- 1/2 cup (120ml) whole milk, warmed
- 1/4 cup (60g) unsalted butter, melted
- 2 large eggs

For the Topping:

- 1/2 cup (115g) unsalted butter
- 1/2 cup (100g) granulated sugar
- 2 tablespoons honey
- 1 tablespoon whole milk
- 1 cup (100g) sliced almonds

For the Filling:

- 1 1/2 cups (360ml) whole milk
- 1/3 cup (65g) granulated sugar
- 3 large egg yolks
- 3 tablespoons cornstarch
- 1 teaspoon vanilla extract
- 1 cup (240ml) heavy cream, whipped

Instructions:

1. Prepare the Dough:

- In a large mixing bowl, combine the flour, sugar, salt, and yeast.
    - Add the warmed milk, melted butter, and eggs to the dry ingredients. Mix until a dough forms.
    - Knead the dough on a floured surface for about 5-7 minutes, or until smooth and elastic.
    - Place the dough in a greased bowl, cover with a clean kitchen towel, and let it rise in a warm place for about 1 hour, or until doubled in size.
2. Prepare the Topping:
    - In a saucepan, melt the butter over medium heat.
    - Stir in the sugar, honey, and milk until well combined.
    - Bring the mixture to a boil, then remove from heat and stir in the sliced almonds. Set aside to cool slightly.
3. Shape and Assemble the Cake:
    - Preheat your oven to 375°F (190°C). Grease a 9x13-inch (23x33cm) baking dish.
    - Punch down the risen dough and transfer it to the prepared baking dish. Press the dough evenly into the bottom of the dish.
    - Spread the almond topping evenly over the dough.
    - Let the cake rise for an additional 20-30 minutes.
4. Bake the Cake:
    - Bake the Bienenstich in the preheated oven for 20-25 minutes, or until golden brown and the edges are slightly crispy.
    - Remove from the oven and let the cake cool completely in the baking dish.
5. Prepare the Filling:
    - In a saucepan, heat the milk over medium heat until it just begins to simmer.
    - In a separate bowl, whisk together the sugar, egg yolks, and cornstarch until smooth and creamy.
    - Gradually pour the warm milk into the egg mixture, whisking constantly to temper the eggs.
    - Return the mixture to the saucepan and cook over medium-low heat, stirring constantly, until it thickens into a custard-like consistency.
    - Remove from heat and stir in the vanilla extract. Let the custard cool completely.
6. Assemble the Cake:
    - Once the cake and custard are cooled, spread the custard evenly over the cooled cake layer.
    - Top the custard layer with the whipped cream, spreading it out evenly.
7. Chill and Serve:

- Refrigerate the assembled Bienenstich for at least 2 hours, or until set.
- Slice the chilled cake into squares and serve chilled.
- Enjoy this delightful German Bee Sting Cake as a special treat for any occasion!

Bienenstich is a classic German dessert consisting of a yeast dough base topped with caramelized almonds and filled with a creamy custard filling. Its name, which translates to "Bee Sting Cake," comes from the idea that the cake's sweetness could attract bees. With its combination of textures and flavors, Bienenstich is sure to be a hit with anyone who tries it!

Kaiserschmarrn (Austria)

Ingredients:

- 4 large eggs, separated
- 1/4 cup (50g) granulated sugar
- 1 cup (240ml) whole milk
- 1 cup (125g) all-purpose flour
- 1/4 teaspoon salt
- 4 tablespoons unsalted butter
- 1/2 cup (75g) raisins (optional)
- Powdered sugar, for dusting
- Fruit compote, applesauce, or jam, for serving (optional)

Instructions:

1. Separate Eggs:
    - Separate the egg whites from the egg yolks, placing them into separate bowls.
2. Prepare Batter:
    - In a mixing bowl, beat the egg yolks with the granulated sugar until pale and creamy.
    - Gradually add the milk, mixing until well combined.
    - Sift the flour and salt into the egg yolk mixture, stirring until smooth and no lumps remain.
3. Whip Egg Whites:
    - In another clean mixing bowl, beat the egg whites with a pinch of salt until stiff peaks form.
4. Fold in Egg Whites:
    - Gently fold the whipped egg whites into the batter until just combined. Be careful not to deflate the mixture.
5. Cooking Kaiserschmarrn:
    - In a large non-stick skillet or frying pan, melt 2 tablespoons of butter over medium heat.
    - Pour half of the batter into the skillet, spreading it out evenly.
    - Sprinkle half of the raisins (if using) over the batter.

- Cook the batter for 3-4 minutes, or until the bottom is golden brown and the edges begin to set.
- Using a spatula, flip the pancake and cook the other side for an additional 3-4 minutes, or until golden brown and cooked through.
- Repeat the process with the remaining batter and raisins, adding more butter to the skillet as needed.

6. Shred Pancakes:
    - Once both pancakes are cooked, use a spatula or fork to shred them into bite-sized pieces directly in the skillet.
7. Finish Cooking:
    - Add the remaining 2 tablespoons of butter to the skillet and continue cooking the shredded pancakes, stirring occasionally, until they are evenly golden brown and slightly crispy.
8. Serve:
    - Transfer the cooked Kaiserschmarrn to serving plates.
    - Dust generously with powdered sugar.
    - Serve warm with fruit compote, applesauce, or jam on the side, if desired.
9. Enjoy:
    - Enjoy this classic Austrian dessert as a comforting treat for breakfast, brunch, or dessert!

Kaiserschmarrn is a beloved Austrian dessert that consists of light and fluffy shredded pancakes, often served with powdered sugar and fruit compote. It's a delightful dish that's perfect for sharing with family and friends.

Alfajores (Argentina)

Ingredients:

For the Cookies:

- 1 cup (225g) unsalted butter, softened
- 1/2 cup (100g) granulated sugar
- 2 large egg yolks
- 1 teaspoon vanilla extract
- 2 cups (250g) all-purpose flour
- 1/2 cup (60g) cornstarch
- 1 teaspoon baking powder
- 1/4 teaspoon salt
- Dulce de leche, for filling

For Coating:

- 1 cup (120g) powdered sugar
- Shredded coconut, for rolling (optional)

Instructions:

1. Prepare Dough:
    - In a large mixing bowl, cream together the softened butter and granulated sugar until light and fluffy.
    - Add the egg yolks one at a time, beating well after each addition.
    - Stir in the vanilla extract until well combined.
2. Combine Dry Ingredients:
    - In a separate bowl, sift together the all-purpose flour, cornstarch, baking powder, and salt.
3. Form Dough:
    - Gradually add the dry ingredients to the wet mixture, mixing until a soft dough forms.

- Gather the dough into a ball, wrap it in plastic wrap, and refrigerate for at least 30 minutes to firm up.
4. Preheat Oven:
   - Preheat your oven to 350°F (175°C). Line a baking sheet with parchment paper.
5. Roll and Cut Dough:
   - On a floured surface, roll out the chilled dough to about 1/4 inch (6mm) thickness.
   - Using a round cookie cutter, cut out cookies and place them on the prepared baking sheet, spacing them about 1 inch (2.5cm) apart.
6. Bake Cookies:
   - Bake the cookies in the preheated oven for 10-12 minutes, or until the edges are lightly golden.
   - Remove from the oven and let the cookies cool completely on a wire rack.
7. Assemble Alfajores:
   - Once the cookies are cooled, spread a dollop of dulce de leche onto the bottom of one cookie.
   - Sandwich with another cookie, pressing gently to adhere.
   - Repeat with the remaining cookies and dulce de leche to form alfajores sandwiches.
8. Coat Alfajores:
   - Roll the edges of the assembled alfajores in shredded coconut, if desired.
   - Dust the tops of the alfajores with powdered sugar.
9. Serve and Enjoy:
   - Serve these delicious Argentinean alfajores as a delightful treat with a cup of coffee or tea.

Alfajores are a classic Argentinean treat consisting of delicate shortbread cookies filled with dulce de leche and often coated with shredded coconut. They are beloved for their melt-in-your-mouth texture and irresistible sweetness, making them a perfect indulgence for any occasion.

Chocotorta (Argentina)

Ingredients:

- 400g chocolate cookies (such as chocolate graham crackers or chocolate digestive biscuits)
- 400g dulce de leche
- 500g cream cheese, softened
- 1 cup (240ml) heavy cream
- 1/4 cup (30g) cocoa powder
- Chocolate shavings or cocoa powder, for garnish (optional)

Instructions:

1. Prepare the Cream Mixture:
   - In a mixing bowl, beat the softened cream cheese until smooth and creamy.
   - Add the heavy cream and cocoa powder to the cream cheese and continue beating until well combined and fluffy. Set aside.
2. Assemble the Chocotorta:
   - In a separate bowl, mix the dulce de leche until smooth and creamy.
   - Spread a thin layer of the dulce de leche on the bottom of a 9x13-inch (23x33cm) baking dish.
   - Dip each chocolate cookie into milk (or coffee for a stronger flavor) and place them in a single layer on top of the dulce de leche, covering the bottom of the dish.
   - Spread a layer of the cream mixture over the cookies.
   - Repeat the layers, alternating between dipped cookies, dulce de leche, and cream mixture, until all ingredients are used, finishing with a layer of cream mixture on top.
3. Chill and Serve:
   - Cover the Chocotorta with plastic wrap and refrigerate for at least 4 hours, or preferably overnight, to allow the flavors to meld and the dessert to set.
   - Before serving, garnish with chocolate shavings or dust with cocoa powder, if desired.
   - Slice and serve the delicious Chocotorta chilled.

Chocotorta is a popular Argentinean no-bake dessert made with layers of chocolate cookies soaked in milk or coffee, dulce de leche, and a creamy filling made from cream cheese and heavy cream. It's a decadent and indulgent treat that's perfect for satisfying any sweet craving!

Turkish Delight (Turkey)

Ingredients:

- 2 cups (400g) granulated sugar
- 1 1/4 cups (300ml) water
- 1/4 cup (60ml) lemon juice
- 1 cup (120g) cornstarch
- 1/4 teaspoon cream of tartar
- 1 1/2 teaspoons rose water (or other flavorings such as orange blossom water or vanilla extract)
- Food coloring (optional)
- Confectioners' sugar, for dusting
- Cornstarch, for dusting

Instructions:

1. Prepare the Sugar Syrup:
    - In a medium saucepan, combine the granulated sugar and water. Stir over medium heat until the sugar has dissolved.
    - Add the lemon juice to the sugar syrup and bring the mixture to a boil. Reduce the heat and let it simmer for about 15 minutes, stirring occasionally, until it reaches the soft-ball stage (about 240°F or 116°C on a candy thermometer).
2. Prepare the Starch Mixture:
    - While the sugar syrup is cooking, in a separate bowl, mix the cornstarch and cream of tartar together.
    - Gradually add 3/4 cup (180ml) of water to the cornstarch mixture, stirring until smooth and well combined.
3. Combine the Mixtures:
    - Once the sugar syrup reaches the desired temperature, slowly pour it into the cornstarch mixture, whisking constantly to prevent lumps from forming.
4. Cook the Mixture:
    - Transfer the combined mixture back to the saucepan and place it over medium-low heat.

- Cook the mixture, stirring constantly, for about 20-25 minutes, or until it becomes thick and translucent.
5. Add Flavorings and Coloring:
    - Once the mixture is thickened, stir in the rose water (or other flavorings) and food coloring, if using. Mix until well combined.
6. Pour and Set:
    - Pour the hot mixture into a lightly greased square baking dish lined with parchment paper.
    - Smooth the surface with a spatula and let it cool at room temperature for a few hours, or until set.
7. Cut and Dust:
    - Once the Turkish delight is set, use a sharp knife to cut it into small squares or rectangles.
    - Dust the cut pieces with a mixture of equal parts confectioners' sugar and cornstarch to prevent sticking.
8. Store and Enjoy:
    - Store the Turkish delight in an airtight container at room temperature for up to two weeks.
    - Enjoy this delightful Turkish treat as a sweet snack or dessert!

Turkish Delight, known as "lokum" in Turkey, is a traditional confection made from sugar, water, and starch, flavored with rose water and often colored with food coloring. It has a chewy texture and is typically dusted with powdered sugar or cornstarch to prevent sticking. It's a beloved sweet treat enjoyed in Turkey and around the world.

Bûche de Noël (France)

Ingredients:

For the Sponge Cake:

- 4 large eggs
- 3/4 cup (150g) granulated sugar
- 1 teaspoon vanilla extract
- 1/2 cup (60g) all-purpose flour
- 1/4 cup (30g) unsweetened cocoa powder
- 1/4 teaspoon salt
- Confectioners' sugar, for dusting

For the Filling:

- 1 cup (240ml) heavy cream
- 2 tablespoons granulated sugar
- 1 teaspoon vanilla extract

For the Chocolate Ganache:

- 6 ounces (170g) semisweet chocolate, chopped
- 1/2 cup (120ml) heavy cream
- 2 tablespoons unsalted butter

For Decoration (Optional):

- Additional whipped cream
- Marzipan mushrooms
- Meringue mushrooms
- Fresh berries
- Confectioners' sugar for snow effect

Instructions:

1. Prepare the Sponge Cake:
   - Preheat your oven to 350°F (180°C). Grease a 15x10-inch (38x25cm) jelly roll pan and line it with parchment paper.
   - In a large mixing bowl, beat the eggs and granulated sugar together until pale and thick, about 5 minutes.
   - Stir in the vanilla extract.
   - In a separate bowl, sift together the flour, cocoa powder, and salt.
   - Gradually fold the dry ingredients into the egg mixture until just combined.
   - Pour the batter into the prepared jelly roll pan and spread it out evenly.
   - Bake in the preheated oven for 10-12 minutes, or until the cake is set and springs back when lightly touched.
2. Roll the Cake:
   - While the cake is still warm, dust a clean kitchen towel generously with confectioners' sugar.
   - Invert the cake onto the prepared towel and carefully peel off the parchment paper.
   - Starting from one of the short ends, gently roll up the cake and towel together into a tight spiral. Place the rolled cake seam side down and let it cool completely.
3. Prepare the Filling:
   - In a mixing bowl, whip the heavy cream, granulated sugar, and vanilla extract together until stiff peaks form.
4. Fill the Cake:
   - Carefully unroll the cooled cake and spread the whipped cream filling evenly over the surface, leaving a small border around the edges.
   - Roll the cake back up without the towel, starting from the same short end as before. Place the rolled cake seam side down on a serving platter.
5. Make the Chocolate Ganache:
   - Place the chopped chocolate in a heatproof bowl.
   - In a small saucepan, heat the heavy cream until it just begins to simmer.
   - Pour the hot cream over the chopped chocolate and let it sit for 1-2 minutes.
   - Add the butter to the bowl and stir the mixture until smooth and glossy.
6. Frost the Cake:
   - Pour the chocolate ganache over the rolled cake, using a spatula to spread it evenly over the surface and sides.

- Use a fork or spatula to create a bark-like texture on the surface of the ganache.
7. Decorate (Optional):
   - Use additional whipped cream to create a snowy effect on top of the log.
   - Decorate with marzipan or meringue mushrooms, fresh berries, and a dusting of confectioners' sugar.
8. Chill and Serve:
   - Refrigerate the Bûche de Noël for at least 1-2 hours, or until the ganache is set.
   - Slice and serve this festive dessert to delight your guests during the holiday season!

Bûche de Noël, or Yule Log, is a classic French dessert enjoyed during the holiday season. This festive cake features a light and airy sponge cake filled with whipped cream, rolled into a log shape, and frosted with chocolate ganache. It's a beautiful and delicious centerpiece for any holiday celebration.

Stroopwafel (Netherlands)

Ingredients:

For the Dough:

- 2 cups (250g) all-purpose flour
- 1/2 cup (100g) granulated sugar
- 1/2 cup (115g) unsalted butter, melted
- 1 large egg
- 1 teaspoon active dry yeast
- 1/4 cup (60ml) lukewarm milk
- 1/2 teaspoon vanilla extract
- 1/4 teaspoon ground cinnamon
- Pinch of salt

For the Caramel Filling (Stroop):

- 1 cup (200g) brown sugar
- 1/2 cup (115g) unsalted butter
- 1/4 cup (60ml) dark corn syrup or golden syrup
- 1 teaspoon ground cinnamon
- 1/4 teaspoon salt

Instructions:

1. Prepare the Dough:
    - In a small bowl, dissolve the yeast in lukewarm milk and let it sit for 5-10 minutes until frothy.
    - In a large mixing bowl, combine the flour, sugar, melted butter, egg, vanilla extract, ground cinnamon, and salt.
    - Add the yeast mixture to the dough and mix until well combined.
    - Knead the dough until it becomes smooth and elastic. If the dough is too sticky, add a little more flour.

- Shape the dough into a ball, cover the bowl with plastic wrap, and let it rest for about 1 hour, or until doubled in size.
2. Make the Caramel Filling (Stroop):
    - In a saucepan, combine the brown sugar, unsalted butter, dark corn syrup (or golden syrup), ground cinnamon, and salt.
    - Cook over medium heat, stirring constantly, until the mixture comes to a boil.
    - Reduce the heat to low and let the mixture simmer for about 5-7 minutes, stirring occasionally, until it thickens slightly.
    - Remove from heat and let the caramel filling cool slightly.
3. Shape and Cook the Stroopwafels:
    - Preheat a stroopwafel iron or pizzelle maker according to the manufacturer's instructions.
    - Divide the rested dough into small balls, about 1 tablespoon each.
    - Place a ball of dough onto the preheated iron and close the lid, pressing down to flatten the dough.
    - Cook the dough for about 1-2 minutes, or until golden brown and crispy.
    - Carefully remove the cooked stroopwafel from the iron and transfer it to a wire rack to cool.
    - While the stroopwafel is still warm, use a sharp knife to carefully slice it in half horizontally to create two thin wafers.
4. Assemble the Stroopwafels:
    - Spread a spoonful of the caramel filling (stroop) onto one of the wafers.
    - Place the other wafer on top and gently press down to sandwich the caramel filling.
5. Serve and Enjoy:
    - Serve the stroopwafels warm or at room temperature.
    - Enjoy these delicious Dutch treats with a cup of coffee or tea for a delightful snack or dessert!

Stroopwafels are a beloved Dutch treat consisting of two thin waffle cookies sandwiched together with a layer of caramel syrup (stroop). They are crispy on the outside, chewy on the inside, and wonderfully sweet and indulgent. These homemade stroopwafels are sure to delight your taste buds!

Pandan Cake (Singapore)

Ingredients:

For the Pandan Paste:

- 1 cup (about 30g) pandan leaves, chopped
- 1/4 cup (60ml) water

For the Cake:

- 1 3/4 cups (220g) cake flour
- 1 teaspoon baking powder
- 1/4 teaspoon salt
- 1/2 cup (120ml) coconut milk
- 1 tablespoon pandan extract (from the pandan paste)
- 1/2 cup (115g) unsalted butter, softened
- 3/4 cup (150g) granulated sugar
- 3 large eggs
- Green food coloring (optional, for a more vibrant color)

For the Glaze (Optional):

- 1/2 cup (60g) powdered sugar
- 1-2 tablespoons coconut milk or water

Instructions:

1. Prepare the Pandan Paste:
   - In a blender or food processor, blend the chopped pandan leaves with water until smooth.
   - Strain the pandan mixture through a fine mesh sieve or cheesecloth to extract the pandan juice. Discard the pulp.
2. Preheat Oven and Prepare Pan:
   - Preheat your oven to 350°F (175°C). Grease and flour a 9-inch (23cm) round cake pan.
3. Make the Cake Batter:

- In a mixing bowl, sift together the cake flour, baking powder, and salt. Set aside.
- In another bowl, combine the coconut milk and pandan extract.
- In a large mixing bowl, cream together the softened butter and granulated sugar until light and fluffy.
- Add the eggs one at a time, beating well after each addition.
- Gradually add the flour mixture to the butter mixture, alternating with the coconut milk mixture, beginning and ending with the flour mixture. Mix until well combined.
- If desired, add a few drops of green food coloring to enhance the color of the cake batter.

4. Bake the Cake:
   - Pour the batter into the prepared cake pan and smooth the top with a spatula.
   - Bake in the preheated oven for 30-35 minutes, or until a toothpick inserted into the center comes out clean.
   - Remove the cake from the oven and let it cool in the pan for 10 minutes before transferring it to a wire rack to cool completely.
5. Make the Glaze (Optional):
   - In a small bowl, whisk together the powdered sugar and coconut milk (or water) until smooth. Adjust the consistency by adding more liquid if needed.
6. Glaze the Cake (Optional):
   - Once the cake has cooled completely, drizzle the glaze over the top of the cake.
   - Allow the glaze to set before slicing and serving.
7. Serve and Enjoy:
   - Slice and serve the pandan cake as a delightful treat for any occasion, accompanied by a cup of tea or coffee.

Pandan cake is a popular Singaporean dessert known for its vibrant green color and fragrant pandan flavor. Made with pandan extract, coconut milk, and a hint of sweetness, this soft and fluffy cake is sure to delight your taste buds with its unique and tropical taste.

Basbousa (Middle East)

Ingredients:

For the Cake:

- 1 1/2 cups (225g) semolina
- 1 cup (200g) granulated sugar
- 1 cup (240ml) plain yogurt
- 1/2 cup (120ml) melted unsalted butter
- 1 teaspoon baking powder
- 1/4 teaspoon baking soda
- 1/4 teaspoon salt
- 1/2 cup (60g) blanched almonds or pine nuts, for garnish (optional)

For the Syrup:

- 1 cup (200g) granulated sugar
- 1 cup (240ml) water
- 1 tablespoon lemon juice
- 1 teaspoon rose water or orange blossom water (optional)

Instructions:

1. Preheat Oven and Prepare Pan:
    - Preheat your oven to 350°F (175°C). Grease a 9x13-inch (23x33cm) baking dish or cake pan.
2. Make the Cake:
    - In a large mixing bowl, combine the semolina, granulated sugar, plain yogurt, melted butter, baking powder, baking soda, and salt. Mix until well combined and smooth.
3. Pour Batter into Pan:
    - Pour the batter into the prepared baking dish and spread it out evenly with a spatula.
4. Score and Garnish (Optional):
    - Use a sharp knife to score the surface of the cake into diamond or square shapes.

- Place a blanched almond or pine nut in the center of each scored shape, if desired, for decoration.
5. Bake the Cake:
    - Bake the basbousa in the preheated oven for 25-30 minutes, or until the top is golden brown and a toothpick inserted into the center comes out clean.
6. Make the Syrup:
    - While the cake is baking, prepare the syrup. In a saucepan, combine the granulated sugar, water, and lemon juice.
    - Bring the mixture to a boil over medium heat, then reduce the heat and let it simmer for about 10-15 minutes, or until slightly thickened.
    - Remove the syrup from the heat and stir in the rose water or orange blossom water, if using. Set aside to cool slightly.
7. Pour Syrup Over Warm Cake:
    - Once the cake is done baking and still warm, evenly pour the warm syrup over the entire surface of the cake.
8. Let the Cake Absorb Syrup:
    - Allow the basbousa to sit for at least 1 hour, or until it has absorbed the syrup and cooled completely.
9. Serve and Enjoy:
    - Cut the basbousa into squares or diamonds along the scored lines.
    - Serve the delicious Middle Eastern basbousa as a sweet treat with a cup of tea or coffee.

Basbousa is a traditional Middle Eastern dessert made from semolina, sugar, yogurt, and butter, flavored with a hint of rose water or orange blossom water. It's a simple yet delicious treat that's perfect for sharing with family and friends during special occasions or gatherings.

Pumpkin Pie (United States)

Ingredients:

For the Pie Crust:

- 1 1/4 cups (155g) all-purpose flour
- 1/2 teaspoon salt
- 1/2 teaspoon granulated sugar
- 1/2 cup (115g) unsalted butter, cold and cut into cubes
- 3-4 tablespoons ice water

For the Pumpkin Filling:

- 1 can (15 ounces) pumpkin puree
- 3/4 cup (150g) packed brown sugar
- 2 large eggs
- 1 cup (240ml) heavy cream
- 1 teaspoon ground cinnamon
- 1/2 teaspoon ground ginger
- 1/4 teaspoon ground nutmeg
- 1/4 teaspoon ground cloves
- 1/2 teaspoon salt

For Whipped Cream (Optional):

- 1 cup (240ml) heavy cream
- 2 tablespoons powdered sugar
- 1/2 teaspoon vanilla extract

Instructions:

1. Prepare the Pie Crust:
    - In a large mixing bowl, combine the flour, salt, and granulated sugar.

- Add the cold cubed butter to the flour mixture. Using a pastry cutter or your fingers, work the butter into the flour until the mixture resembles coarse crumbs.
- Gradually add the ice water, 1 tablespoon at a time, mixing with a fork until the dough comes together.
- Shape the dough into a disk, wrap it in plastic wrap, and refrigerate for at least 30 minutes.

2. Roll Out the Pie Crust:
   - Preheat your oven to 375°F (190°C).
   - On a lightly floured surface, roll out the chilled dough into a circle about 12 inches (30cm) in diameter.
   - Carefully transfer the rolled-out dough to a 9-inch (23cm) pie dish. Trim any excess dough from the edges and crimp the edges as desired.
3. Prepare the Pumpkin Filling:
   - In a large mixing bowl, whisk together the pumpkin puree, brown sugar, eggs, heavy cream, ground cinnamon, ground ginger, ground nutmeg, ground cloves, and salt until smooth and well combined.
4. Fill the Pie Crust:
   - Pour the pumpkin filling into the prepared pie crust, spreading it out evenly.
5. Bake the Pie:
   - Place the pie in the preheated oven and bake for 45-50 minutes, or until the filling is set and the crust is golden brown.
   - If the crust edges start to brown too quickly, you can cover them with aluminum foil or a pie shield.
6. Cool and Serve:
   - Once baked, remove the pie from the oven and let it cool completely on a wire rack before slicing.
   - Serve slices of pumpkin pie with whipped cream, if desired.

For Whipped Cream (Optional):

1. Prepare Whipped Cream:
   - In a mixing bowl, beat the heavy cream, powdered sugar, and vanilla extract together until stiff peaks form.
   - Dollop or pipe the whipped cream onto slices of pumpkin pie before serving.

Pumpkin pie is a classic American dessert, especially popular during the fall and Thanksgiving season. It features a spiced pumpkin filling baked in a flaky pie crust, resulting in a rich and comforting dessert that's perfect for sharing with loved ones.

Maple Taffy (Canada)

Ingredients:

- Pure maple syrup (about 1 cup per serving)
- Clean snow or crushed ice

Equipment:

- Candy thermometer
- Wooden popsicle sticks or clean twigs

Instructions:

1. Prepare Snow or Ice:
   - If using snow, make sure it's clean and fresh. If using crushed ice, pack it into a shallow baking dish or pan.
2. Heat Maple Syrup:
   - In a small saucepan, heat the maple syrup over medium-high heat, stirring occasionally. Attach a candy thermometer to the side of the saucepan.
3. Boil Maple Syrup:
   - Bring the maple syrup to a boil and continue boiling until it reaches the soft ball stage, which is around 235°F to 240°F (113°C to 116°C). This stage is important for the taffy to set properly.
4. Test the Syrup:
   - To test if the syrup has reached the soft ball stage, drop a small amount of syrup into a cup of cold water. It should form a soft ball that flattens when removed from the water.
5. Pour Maple Syrup onto Snow or Ice:
   - Once the maple syrup has reached the desired temperature, immediately remove it from the heat.
   - Carefully pour the hot maple syrup in thin lines or pools onto the clean snow or crushed ice. Leave some space between each pour to allow the taffy to set.
6. Insert Sticks:

- Quickly insert wooden popsicle sticks or clean twigs into the hot maple syrup pools before they cool and harden.
7. Let Set:
    - Allow the maple taffy to set for a few seconds to a minute, depending on the temperature of the snow or ice. The taffy will cool and harden around the sticks.
8. Enjoy:
    - Once the maple taffy has set, lift it from the snow or ice using the sticks and enjoy the sweet and chewy treat!

Maple taffy, also known as "maple syrup on snow," is a classic Canadian treat made by pouring hot maple syrup onto clean snow or crushed ice. As the syrup cools and hardens, it forms a chewy taffy-like candy that's delightfully sweet and bursting with maple flavor. It's a fun and festive treat enjoyed during the winter months, especially during maple syrup season in Canada.

Peach Melba (Australia)

Ingredients:

For the Poached Peaches:

- 4 ripe peaches, peeled, pitted, and halved
- 1 cup (240ml) water
- 1/2 cup (100g) granulated sugar
- 1 vanilla bean, split lengthwise (optional)
- Juice of 1 lemon

For the Raspberry Sauce:

- 1 1/2 cups (180g) fresh or frozen raspberries
- 1/4 cup (50g) granulated sugar
- 1 tablespoon lemon juice

For Serving:

- Vanilla ice cream
- Fresh raspberries, for garnish (optional)
- Mint leaves, for garnish (optional)

Instructions:

1. Prepare the Poached Peaches:
   - In a saucepan, combine the water, granulated sugar, and split vanilla bean (if using). Bring the mixture to a simmer over medium heat, stirring until the sugar is dissolved.
   - Add the peach halves and lemon juice to the simmering syrup. Cook for about 5-7 minutes, or until the peaches are tender but still hold their shape.
   - Remove the peaches from the syrup using a slotted spoon and let them cool slightly. Reserve the poaching liquid for later use.
2. Make the Raspberry Sauce:
   - In a blender or food processor, puree the raspberries until smooth.

- Strain the raspberry puree through a fine mesh sieve to remove the seeds.
- In a small saucepan, combine the strained raspberry puree, granulated sugar, and lemon juice. Cook over medium heat, stirring constantly, until the sugar is dissolved and the sauce has slightly thickened. Remove from heat and let it cool.
3. Assemble the Peach Melba:
    - Place a scoop of vanilla ice cream in each serving bowl or dish.
    - Arrange the poached peach halves on top of the ice cream.
    - Drizzle the raspberry sauce over the peaches and ice cream.
4. Garnish and Serve:
    - Garnish the Peach Melba with fresh raspberries and mint leaves, if desired.
    - Serve immediately and enjoy this delightful Australian dessert!

Peach Melba is a classic Australian dessert created by renowned chef Auguste Escoffier in the late 19th century to honor the Australian opera singer Nellie Melba. It features poached peaches served with vanilla ice cream and raspberry sauce. This elegant and refreshing dessert is perfect for summer gatherings and special occasions, showcasing the beautiful flavors of fresh peaches and raspberries.

Banoffee Pie (United Kingdom)

Ingredients:

For the Crust:

- 1 1/2 cups (150g) graham cracker crumbs (or digestive biscuit crumbs)
- 1/3 cup (75g) unsalted butter, melted

For the Toffee Filling:

- 1 can (14 ounces or 397g) sweetened condensed milk (or dulce de leche)

For the Banana Layer:

- 3 ripe bananas, sliced

For the Whipped Cream Topping:

- 1 cup (240ml) heavy cream
- 2 tablespoons powdered sugar
- 1/2 teaspoon vanilla extract

For Garnish (Optional):

- Grated chocolate or cocoa powder
- Sliced bananas

Instructions:

1. Prepare the Crust:
    - In a mixing bowl, combine the graham cracker crumbs and melted butter until the crumbs are evenly moistened.
    - Press the mixture firmly into the bottom and up the sides of a 9-inch (23cm) pie dish. Use the back of a spoon or the bottom of a glass to help pack the crust tightly.

- Chill the crust in the refrigerator for at least 30 minutes to firm up.
2. Make the Toffee Filling:
    - If using sweetened condensed milk, pour it into a heatproof bowl. Place the bowl over a pot of simmering water (double boiler method) and cook, stirring occasionally, for 1-2 hours or until the condensed milk caramelizes and turns into a thick toffee. Alternatively, you can use pre-made dulce de leche.
    - Once the toffee is ready, pour it into the chilled crust and spread it out evenly. Let it cool completely.
3. Layer the Bananas:
    - Arrange the sliced bananas over the toffee layer in the pie crust.
4. Prepare the Whipped Cream:
    - In a mixing bowl, beat the heavy cream, powdered sugar, and vanilla extract together until stiff peaks form.
5. Top the Pie:
    - Spread the whipped cream over the banana layer, covering the entire surface of the pie.
6. Garnish (Optional):
    - Sprinkle grated chocolate or cocoa powder over the whipped cream.
    - Add additional sliced bananas on top for decoration if desired.
7. Chill and Serve:
    - Refrigerate the Banoffee Pie for at least 2 hours, or until set.
    - Slice and serve this indulgent dessert cold, enjoying the layers of creamy toffee, sweet bananas, and fluffy whipped cream.

Banoffee Pie is a classic British dessert consisting of a crumbly crust, a layer of toffee (made from sweetened condensed milk), sliced bananas, and whipped cream. It's a deliciously indulgent treat that's perfect for any occasion, from casual gatherings to special celebrations.

Panna Cotta (Italy)

Ingredients:

- 2 cups (480ml) heavy cream
- 1/2 cup (120ml) whole milk
- 1/2 cup (100g) granulated sugar
- 2 teaspoons vanilla extract
- 2 1/4 teaspoons powdered gelatin
- 3 tablespoons cold water

For the Raspberry Sauce (Optional):

- 1 cup (120g) fresh or frozen raspberries
- 2-3 tablespoons granulated sugar
- 1 tablespoon lemon juice

For Garnish (Optional):

- Fresh berries
- Mint leaves
- Honey
- Balsamic reduction

Instructions:

1. Prepare Gelatin Mixture:
   - In a small bowl, sprinkle the powdered gelatin over the cold water. Let it sit for about 5-10 minutes to soften.
2. Heat Cream and Milk:
   - In a saucepan, combine the heavy cream, whole milk, and granulated sugar. Heat the mixture over medium heat, stirring occasionally, until it begins to steam and the sugar has dissolved. Do not boil.
3. Combine Gelatin and Cream Mixture:
   - Once the cream mixture is heated, remove it from the heat.

- Add the softened gelatin to the warm cream mixture and whisk until the gelatin is completely dissolved.
4. Add Vanilla:
   - Stir in the vanilla extract until well combined.
5. Pour into Molds:
   - Divide the panna cotta mixture among individual serving dishes or ramekins.
   - Allow the panna cotta to cool slightly at room temperature before covering and transferring to the refrigerator to chill for at least 4 hours, or until set.
6. Prepare Raspberry Sauce (Optional):
   - In a small saucepan, combine the raspberries, granulated sugar, and lemon juice.
   - Cook the mixture over medium heat, stirring occasionally, until the raspberries break down and the sauce thickens slightly, about 5-7 minutes.
   - Remove from heat and let the sauce cool. Strain through a fine mesh sieve to remove the seeds, if desired.
7. Serve:
   - Once the panna cotta is set, unmold onto serving plates by running a knife around the edge of each ramekin and inverting onto a plate. Alternatively, serve directly in the serving dishes.
   - Drizzle with raspberry sauce, if using, and garnish with fresh berries, mint leaves, a drizzle of honey, or a balsamic reduction, if desired.

Panna Cotta is a classic Italian dessert known for its silky smooth texture and rich flavor. Made with cream, milk, sugar, and gelatin, it's a simple yet elegant dessert that can be served on its own or paired with a variety of toppings, sauces, and garnishes.

Sufganiyah (Israel)

Ingredients:

For the Dough:

- 2 1/4 teaspoons (1 packet) active dry yeast
- 1/4 cup (60ml) warm water
- 2 tablespoons granulated sugar, plus extra for rolling
- 2 1/2 - 3 cups (315-375g) all-purpose flour
- 1/2 cup (120ml) milk, warmed
- 2 large eggs
- 2 tablespoons unsalted butter, softened
- 1/2 teaspoon salt
- Vegetable oil, for frying

For the Filling:

- Fruit jam (such as raspberry, strawberry, or apricot)
- Powdered sugar, for dusting

Instructions:

1. Activate the Yeast:
    - In a small bowl, dissolve the yeast and 1 tablespoon of sugar in warm water. Let it sit for about 5-10 minutes, or until frothy.
2. Make the Dough:
    - In a large mixing bowl or the bowl of a stand mixer fitted with a dough hook, combine 2 1/2 cups of flour, remaining tablespoon of sugar, warm milk, eggs, softened butter, salt, and activated yeast mixture.
    - Mix until a soft dough forms. If the dough is too sticky, gradually add more flour, 1 tablespoon at a time, until the dough pulls away from the sides of the bowl.
3. Knead the Dough:

- Turn the dough out onto a lightly floured surface and knead it for about 5-7 minutes, or until it becomes smooth and elastic. Alternatively, knead the dough in the stand mixer for the same amount of time.
4. First Rise:
    - Place the dough in a greased bowl, cover it with a clean kitchen towel or plastic wrap, and let it rise in a warm, draft-free place for about 1-1.5 hours, or until doubled in size.
5. Shape and Fill the Sufganiyot:
    - After the dough has risen, punch it down and turn it out onto a lightly floured surface.
    - Roll out the dough to about 1/4-inch (6mm) thickness.
    - Using a round cookie cutter or drinking glass, cut out circles of dough.
    - Place a small amount of fruit jam in the center of half of the circles.
    - Brush the edges of the jam-topped circles with water.
    - Top each jam-topped circle with a plain circle of dough and press the edges together to seal, forming filled doughnuts.
6. Second Rise:
    - Place the filled doughnuts on a lightly floured baking sheet, cover them with a clean kitchen towel or plastic wrap, and let them rise for another 30-45 minutes, or until slightly puffed.
7. Fry the Sufganiyot:
    - Heat vegetable oil in a deep fryer or large pot to 350°F (175°C).
    - Carefully place a few sufganiyot in the hot oil, being careful not to overcrowd the pot.
    - Fry the sufganiyot for about 1-2 minutes per side, or until golden brown and puffed.
    - Use a slotted spoon or spider strainer to transfer the fried sufganiyot to a paper towel-lined baking sheet to drain excess oil.
8. Fill and Serve:
    - Once the sufganiyot have cooled slightly, dust them with powdered sugar.
    - Fill a piping bag fitted with a small tip with additional fruit jam.
    - Insert the tip of the piping bag into the side of each sufganiyah and squeeze to fill with jam.
    - Serve the sufganiyot warm or at room temperature, and enjoy this delicious Hanukkah treat!

Sufganiyah is a traditional Jewish dessert enjoyed during the Hanukkah festival. These jelly-filled doughnuts are typically fried until golden brown and puffed, then filled with fruit jam and dusted with powdered sugar. They are a deliciously sweet and festive treat that's perfect for celebrating the holiday season.

www.ingramcontent.com/pod-product-compliance
Lightning Source LLC
LaVergne TN
LVHW081555060526
838201LV00054B/1894